6/2024

Buon Viag

A great summer read

by your neighborhood

author in The Lakes

Enjoy a vicarious voyage

across many regions with

adventure and cultural

genius. Discover the

generosity of those

magnifico Italianos!

Benedizione + Many Mondi

Grazi-Thank you for reviews

& passing it on

The Italian Spirit

In the World of Italy

A Lighthearted Leap across the boot of Italy through the Eyes of an Italian American

Nancy Mondi

The Italian Spirit
In The World of Italy

Cover design & photographs: Nancy Mondi

italianmondi@hotmail.com

https://italiansworld.com

ISBN: 978-1-66788-863-7

The Italian Spirit in The World of Italy

A Lighthearted leap across the boot of Italy through the eyes
of an Italian American. Italians capture your heart through their vibrant acts
of Divine faith, family, and cultural values.

Italian Spirit

In the World of Italy

"How wonderful, thank you, thank you for loving so much my COUNTRY, ITALY!!! ...Amazing Book!

—Rita A,. Lake Como Tour Guide, Italy

"The Italian Spirit rekindled my desire to visit Italy." **—Cindy M.,CO**

"You have captured how immediately friendly Italians are, which makes you feel happy when you're welcome to join them in their workplace and homes. A Nonfiction Narrative that reads like a novel with poetic nature. "

—Reese S.,MO

4.5 STARS****+ "Compelling, Creative Travel Memoir - One wants to promptly be packing their bags for a getaway to catch a flight to Milan, Florence, Rome, or Venice." **—Alice H, CA**

"Witty and adventurous, Italian ancestry, family and culture that's close to heart and draws you into their Divine Faith and inspiration." **—Angelo B., IL**

Table of Contents

Italy Regional

Trentino
South
Tyrol
Friuli
Venezia
Giulia
Lombardy
Veneto
Piedmont
Emilia
Romagna
Liguria
Marche
Tuscany
Umbria
Lazio
Abruzzo
Molise
Apulia
Campania
Basilicata
Sardinia
Calabria
Sicily

Acknowledgments

To the many Italians who gave their time with tremendous generosity and care. To those who helped share their work and interests, even just allowing me to observe like a fly on the wall. Grazie Mille!

To Ann K. who generously supported me with her time for countless hours over a year on and off. I'll forever be grateful.

Many thanks to the enthusiastic friends and associates who encouraged, inspired, and kept me going.

For Jocelyn Vollmar, spiritual sister, a legacy of San Francisco Ballet, ballerina, educator, and poet, who kept me inspired in writing, ballet, and consoling through sad times. Bless her guardian angel soul.

My appreciation to family members who provided ancestry research.

For the opportunity to travel to Italy many times over the years with my husband, Raymond, and his unending support in finally getting the book done.

In honor of my Dad, Vincent Dominick Mondy, and Mom, Madeline Josephine who due to health, had to cancel their tickets to join me in Italy years ago. For all the memorable family events and history you provided.

May your spirits fly high with joy over all of my Italian journeys and God bless your souls.

Introduction

There's more to Italy than Tuscany, Mafia, and linguini.

Hear voices singing an opera *aria* in poetic Italian language, feel the pull of mountain roads winding to Bellagio, the soothing natural spring waters of a *terme*, the spas of Roman baths, taste the flavor of Stracciatella gelato as it melts on your tongue, and capture the aroma of Bolognese sauce simmering outside a trattoria.

The Italian Spirit sings of creative genius, generosity, and humility, transforming my life forever. The nature of Italians with vibrant everyday lives demonstrates their faith in the Divine and captures your heart. Take a lighthearted leap across the boot of Italy for adventures in travel.

Basta! Enough!

In sixth grade at Saint Pius X Catholic School, Aurora, Colorado, a suburb of Denver, I found my fascination with Italy began in the little school library. Our class assignment was to write a term paper on any subject. The day I passed down the library aisles of shelves and came across a particular book, without a clue as to what my term paper subject would be, a large volume on Italian Renaissance Art leaped off the library shelf like Divine destiny. The gorgeous pictures of art and sculpture enchanted me and became my inspired subject as an Italian American. I was twelve years of age.

I realized the narrow views of Americans regarding Italian culture in my teens. M*y desire is to* break away from the images of Mafia stereotypes after seeing *The Godfather* film. The media glamorizes Mafia bosses and gangsters as if many Italian American families are in the crime business when only a fraction of 1% of Italians, mostly Sicilian are involved.

Fast forward to seeing the film, *A Room with a View* in the late 1980s, a romantic love story set in the artistic beauty of Florence, which made me doggedly determined to visit Italy. Distraught by a recent boyfriend breakup whom I thought was the one in my thirties, I was undeterred and driven to overcome my fears and pursue my magnificent obsession with all things Italian. I was not a woman of independent means and prayed not to become forlorn or soppy traveling alone into romantic nature. Just eight months later my magnificent journey takes flight.

Over the next twenty-plus years, I discovered a cornucopia in Italy's twenty varied regions, each as distinctive as the next. My life-transforming adventures and determination dancing across the boot, while in search of ancestry, helped me discover their deeper connection to faith, family, and cultural values. The endless color and flavors of infinite riches inspire me like nothing else to form a cultural connection. Gather a taste of Italy through the eyes of a child, with Italian wisdom through the ages.

"The world is a book and those who do not travel, read only one page." -- St. Augustine

I resisted the traditional roles of housewife and motherhood amongst seven siblings, often babysitting in my early teens. With introspection observing how their families nurture loyalty, trust, and *il dolce far niente,* the sweetness of doing nothing, I found myself drawn to the Italian family culture and creative genius near mid-life years. After all the Roman conquests throughout history, they understand family to be of utmost priority. Devotion to the Divine above all gave me a greater sense of life's purpose with a window view into the essence of being Italian.

I was blessed with many aspects of the American dream, yet still yearned for something that resonated with conviction throughout my life. From the richness of Renaissance Art and culture to lingering in simple country life, recognizing the happiness of Italian families living a richer, yet simpler way of life, transformed my life; each time bringing a piece of Italy back home and a sense of peace closer to my heart. My roots keep calling me to return, renew my spirit, and discover more of the secrets to happiness in Italian life.

The most natural step of sharing my passion for "the Italian way" evolved into writing. Italians' endearing and engaging manner evokes in me the desire to discover their elusive yet formidable spirit, heart, and soul for tradition and culture. Why is no small wonder as these passages will reveal.

Andiamo! Let's Go!

Chapter 1

La Mia Famiglia, Mondi

Growing up in a large Roman Catholic Family, spaghetti was an automatic meal two to three times a week. Dad would not venture to new flavors and styles of cuisine. So, it was Spaghetti and Meatballs, Rigatoni and Meatballs, Spaghetti and Italian Sausage, Lasagna, Spaghetti and Chicken Cacciatore, but mostly Spaghetti and Meatballs. Fried chicken and "leather steak" were Dad's American favorites on the days off from pasta.

Mama Madeline, let the sauce with seasonings simmer at least six hours or it wasn't the real thing with the right flavor. Hers was the sauce of mountain villages and the working class. *Nonna,* Grandma Antonia Mondi, age three, immigrated to America in the late 1890s from Napoli to New York with her Mother *Bisnonna*, Maria Piccoli. Grandma Antonia married Dominic Mondy and delivered 13 *bambini* in Pennsylvania.

Nonna Grandma Antonia shared her recipe with my Mama Madeline. *Nonna* passed on the Old-World Italian recipe thick in tomatoes, to my mom, Madeline. All day and into the evening, the aroma of tomato sauce simmering and the flavors permeated everywhere in our home, and I thought this was the stuff of every family meal.

Front to back-Dad Vincent with brothers, my Uncles Nick and Joe

Nonna Antonia, Buon Compleanno, birthday with her children's families
My father Vincent, mid-table left leaning into light with pompadour

Mama would take many cans of tomato paste plopped into a stewing pot, enough for a small army. Even with seven of us kids, there was always enough for last-minute invites or friends visiting. Dad would often bring home stray airmen from work at Lowry Air Force Base so they could share in our home-cooked meals. I remember some from India, Italy, and all over the United States. We called them "zoomies" or flyboys and in the Beatle era, their buzz cuts were not cool to us kids.

A trio of Italian soldiers came over and said to Mama, "you rest, we want to fix'a spaghetti meal the way'a we do at home'a in Italy." What a delight and treat it turned out to be for our family with such an act of kindness and heartwarming care. I realize now that Dad was simply carrying on the tradition of Italian hospitality. At the Mondi home, this was our version of Sunday family feasts, usually for ten or more as if we were in the old country, outdoors on the long wooden tables. We even had China, silver, and crystal over a white tablecloth crocheted by my Slovenian, maternal grandmother.

Dad was a nice 'a meatball maker. This was his "specialty," he would say with a broad-faced grin, biting his tongue. It was an occasion around our house to see him take a giant bowl of raw ground beef, add in his ingredients of breadcrumbs and eggs, seasonings strong in oregano and knead the squishy red substance into just the perfect consistency, rolling little balls in his hands. He made it a show with this Italian American tradition.

Mama boiled the spaghetti or rigatoni until limp and soggy. This is the way Dad expected it. Not until I reached my thirties did I learn from a well-traveled film producer (not Italian but Jewish) that *il dente*, firmer pasta was the true Italian way of better texture and enhancing flavor.

Dad's most dramatic time was at the dinner table. It wasn't so rare that a utensil would set flight across the table with his taking aim at one of my four brothers engaged in trouble-making stints that day. He'd become enraged after finding out during dinner that brother Jim was again launching a metal ball, not a meatball, from an M-80 firework canon that he made about the size of a zucchini.

Or Dad could flip out about something annoying him from the week before. Those were evenings I was happy to be away at ballet rehearsal. We never knew whether we'd be joking or avoiding catastrophe at the dinner table, but we always had plenty to eat, laughing under the table at Dad's explosive expressions. We could see it simmering. Dad was brought up in the drama of an extremely expressive, temper's flaring Italian home of fourteen children, in poverty. His Dad Dominic provided spankings as regular fare and Dad was pre-wired and determined to carry on the disciplinary tradition. Growing up, he and his brothers often walked the train tracks to find any form of food. Rabbit, squirrel, or squab was the best they could do when it was found.

Enrolling in the Air Force and receiving regular meals with a roof over his head was pure luxury. While stationed in Denver Dad met Mom at a local club The Brass Rail, and they both loved ballroom dancing together at Lowry Officer's Club, Elitch Gardens in Denver, and The Broadmoor Resort in Colorado Springs for over 60 years.

Even in our humble home, I felt blessed, to share in a close-knit family. We siblings usually stuck together in defense of any disturbance. I was happiest when dancing to a piano, invented by an Italian, in ballet class, founded by the Italian Court in the 15th Century, and peacefully attending Mass at St. Pius X Catholic Church on Sundays.

Sunday afternoons we'd often load up and drive off to Collaci's Ristorante, in Louisville, "Louieville", as we endearingly called the then tiny little town near Boulder, CO at the base of the Flatirons of the Rocky Mountains. Louisville was not your eco hipster town like Boulder. Boulder is home to Colorado University and the sixties hippie movement. Even back in the seventies, we called Boulder residents, tree huggers, and granola heads.

Its neighbor, Louisville today boasts being one of America's top small towns to live. An hour's drive across Denver from our suburban home of Aurora in the fifties was quite a trek for a meal in those days with a family of eight or nine.

Collacci's was a family-style restaurant founded in the fifties by Anthony Colacci who opened his own restaurant after serving two years in the army in 1946. Relationship frayed; Anthony stormed out of his father Mike's Blue Parrot Restaurant. The pasta clan feud endured. My father, Vicenzo knew the makings of simple, authentic, and cheap Italian fare with nine mouths to feed. Red and white checkered tablecloths, mixed salads, anti-pasta, and bowls of spaghetti warmed our tummies as we bellied up to the table. Colacci's restaurant survived till the early 2000s and Blue Parrot, 98 years till January 2017.

Yes, somewhere during those formative years, I felt it was special being Italian American. We struggled with seven kids' mouths to feed in our suburban neighborhood outside of Denver. Many other kids didn't have hand-me-downs, often getting new toys and weekly allowances. Yet I was given opportunities to go to parochial school and join a ballet company since Dad worked three jobs. First with the U.S. Postal Service, second a painting contract business, and third Army/Navy surplus sales.

I didn't even dream it possible when I grew up to visit this far-off-land of Italy that my grandmother fondly referred to as *il paese vecchio*, old country. We would intently listen because she was as tough, sometimes tougher than Dad, shouting out in an equally gruff voice, "Gett'a to bed now'a like your father said!" Grandma Antonia had a saying when she did not approve. "God-da knows." When Grandpa Dominic was asked a question, he could not answer, he'd say, ask "God-da knows."

Speaking Italian was discouraged, unfortunately, rather than being invited into our home, which was the case in many Italian immigrant homes. The foresight to maintain Italian as a second language did not exist. Discrimination was rampant and feared as with other ethnic groups. That is with twenty million Italians representing over 6% of the United States population. A desire to speak proper, or at least good English to blend as an All-American became their number one priority to them.

Few schools offered the Italian language for the following generations. From age five to ten, some Sundays were spent with Aunts and Uncles in the Denver area on my mother's side of the family-- she's Slovenian. Uncle Lou had a basement loaded with animals shot and stuffed, up on the walls. Everything from mountain lions to geese. Sometimes the beastly kind like the bear's head "creeped" me out.

Some of the greatest fun we had in Uncle Lou's basement, Mom's brother, was with the pinball machine, like bowling with a puck down a standing shuffle alley board. We would send a puck hurling down shuffle alley, across metal pins on the surface that caused the bowling pins to fold up and disappear instead of being knocked over. I remember being so little that I had to stand on a stool and push the puck with all my might in hopes of getting the pinball bells ringing and lights flashing. Our getaway in the basement from the adults with Cousin Lou Junior was as exciting as an amusement park.

Aunt Rose, Mom's sister, also lived across town in North Denver and had a 45 RPM player with a few choice records. Our favorite 45RPM to play a thousand times over was Harry Belafonte's *Day-O*. My brothers and I would belt out "Day-O" all day long. "Daylight Come and we won't go home" we'd sing out, hoping we wouldn't have to go home to Dad's temper.

I used to think as a child that my father was nuts for cursing and shouting out opinions while reading bad news from the evening newspaper in his easy chair with a bourbon and club soda in hand. Dad would holler, "Those b….ds doing that sh... What's the world coming to?" He would read a snippet of a story out loud from the daily news and argue with himself afterward. He played all the roles as if he were the town crier to an audience in an Italian Piazza or a group of old men who sat around daily on the Piazza benches under shade trees. This was not an occasional outburst, this was daily.

In the parody, I realized Dad was merely characterizing an Italian tradition practiced by his father and grandfather. He just didn't have the town piazza to shout it out with other old guys, opinion makers that discussed news around the square.

Nor did he have the time with seven children always trying to figure a way to outsmart him with wisecracks and practical jokes. I understand some of his impulses now. Dad had eight others with Mom to provide for us as his first thought each day. He was always out the door early and working late extra jobs. I even find myself today caught in the same madness shouting back at the television news or Ray, my husband when they report preposterous claims and we're left digging for the truth.

Italians have the instinct for trust to invite near strangers to a family meal. They have also preserved a gene pool of strikingly attractive features. Just look around you on the streets of Italy. The chiseled faces of men, *Bellissimo,* and the bloodline of athletic gladiators. Pick any American athletic sport and you're likely to find an Italian on the roster. Many women display exaggerated female beauty features, curves, and fashions.

In Italy, the thread of tightly knit communities serves for good reason. Families can maintain a trust and loyalty within the familiar walls of their town. Piazzas serve as the community gathering place and *passeggiate,* evening strolls are daily practice to see your neighbor. This practice has unintended, *bella* consequences for people with chiseled, attractive, and strong features.

Today the family trade is still handed down and weaved through generations. Artistic craftsmanship of refinishing a wooden gondola, gilded door, or tanning and cutting leather is learned and passed on as a highly respected living. Service positions flourish with pride and joy from the waiter to the hairstylist. They understand the virtue of humility makes for some of the greatest saints.

Growing up with the family joy of the fifties and sixties, gave me a privileged feeling even in a lower-middle-class family of seven children. Yes, somewhere during my formative years, I realized I was different being Italian American, maybe even special. I knew we were less fortunate in our suburban neighborhood outside of Denver. Mom and Dad managed with very few luxuries, yet they provided us with special out-to-dinner evenings at Collacci's or summer spa vacations, in Glenwood Springs, Colorado near Aspen, long before they became fashionable, and little did I realize then, just like the tradition of Roman baths.

My enchantment with Italy is like a dance that reflects tradition, choreographed in modern times. Italians think nothing of staging performances on an ancient structure, still useful for a Puccini Opera today. They do not question their way of life, rooted in centuries old practice. Italians flourish in their history and mold it into modern life as if sculpting marble, artistically blending contemporary rituals into their world. Faith, family, and community provide a sense of purpose in their lives.

Italians are endowed with gifted artisan skills. Whether weaving threads of a tapestry a thousand years old in the Vatican, painting gold leaf on a Renaissance door for renovation, tanning leather, and dyeing with extraordinary methods that make you ponder, is that truly leather? A vibrant spirit for maintaining their esteem, integrity in handcrafting, and family tradition is evident and still blossoming.

Growing, picking, and crushing grapes at Fall's harvest in a family vineyard, there is still a glowing countenance in the tradition of agricultural and creative trades, working with their talented hands, passed down through generations within a family. Even with the man who repairs streets replacing cobblestones and taps the stones into place -- such deliberate and concentrated posture. Italians have master tradesmen, special niche industries, and artisans highly respected by their peers. They are approximately 70% of Italy's most productive sector of the workforce today.

These are qualities and skills sadly lacking in our American society. Today's tradesmen are often categorized as blue-collar workers and respect has faded in America's landscape since white collar, college-educated work is viewed as the more admirable line of business. Working with your hands is given less respect in the United States unless you're a fine artist.

Most everything is outsourced with cheap foreign labor. It's fair to say we have driven the discipline of a hard day's physical labor out of even middle-class Americans. Do not be mistaken, I am a very proud American, which gives me hope in a resurgence back to basics with handcraft, service trades, and local manufacturing.

Creative imagination for children is disappearing due to television, computers, and digital media dominating social interaction. Montessori schools have it right in their curriculum of integrated subjects by founder Maria Montessori another Italian.

I hope American culture, can reawaken the need for handwork and creative genius, stimulated through moments of quiet imagination. Quiet downtime has taken on a form of punishment. Art programs and physical education stimulate the creative brain.

After numerous ventures to Italy, I realize we all share a kinship from whatever country of origin. My heart and spirit soar with gratitude for all the blessings Italy and its people have provided us with their rich cultural history.

Whether in the streets of Rome, in the scenic Umbrian hills to the North, Abruzzo's rustic charm or Mediterranean seaside serenity, Italian's speak a language I understand, learning through impressions and circumstance. My heart delights in their vibrant portrayals of daily living. How the antique restorer goes about painting gold leaf on a panel or families gleefully join in the many community piazza festivals.

Italian families even discouraged marrying outside of their region in the past to prevent losing local traditions and community loyalty. My observation is seeing some of the most significant numbers of beautiful people throughout their country -- just look around you. Italian community spirit reigns to maintain a trust and loyalty within the familiar walls of their towns and villages, especially at *piazza* gatherings, *passeggiate*, and *festa,* festivals.

Tarantella dancers and musicians in traditional costume

Chapter 2

Ancestry in Abruzzo -- Wherefore Art Thou Ancestors?

Open my heart and you will see, Graved inside of it, Italy.
—Robert Browning

During the Spring, *La Primavera*, we traverse Italy in a Fiat Punto, making our journey from Perugia to Pesaro and then south along the Adriatic Coast toward Abruzzo. The sea is azure blue, so clean and alluring. The purity of the air and smell of salt water and *pesce*, fish gives me a dramatic sense of man's history through the ages in this land. As the waves of the sea crash and spray up into the air, outlines of ancient gods form in the mist. Visions of Neptune emerge, rising out of the Adriatic and Ionian Seas that separate Italy from Greece. Still after told and untold centuries, the sea and sand are remarkably unspoiled.

My family lost track of our ancestral records. Relatives indicated Perugia, Umbria and Scopoli, Abruzzo. Further research years later revealed my grandparents and great grandparents spanned across the three regions of Umbria, Abruzzo, and LaMarche.

After a delightful day in the university city of Perugia, Umbria, home of the chocolate *baci* kisses, with not a single Sigismondi (shortened to Mondi at Ellis) to be found, the destination becomes Scopoli, Abruzzo. My great grandmother's name is Serafina Bocci whom I discover long after, was from Perugia, so Bocci would be the name to research.

My ongoing quest is the birthplace of my grandparents. Not knowing exactly where the town of Scopoli, Abruzzo is, we make this journey a leap of faith. Feelings of intrigue and an indescribable fear of the unknown sit next to me. Abruzzo is positioned between two of God's most magnificent wonders. Bordered east by the Adriatic Sea and hugging the *Apennino* Mountains, this is a land for farmers and shepherds, and a sea for fishermen. Here, clinging hill towns appear with olive trees and vineyards reaching down to the sea. This expanse of forest and sea was home to both grandpa *Nonno*, Dominic Sigismondi, and grandma *Nonna* Antonia. Their childhood was surrounded by nature's spectacular scenery highlighting Italy's *Gran Sasso*, the highest peak south of The Alps.

Craving a deeper connection to these Bella beautiful, people in a Bella land makes the journey that much sweeter as I come to understand the creative instincts that course through my veins. Little fishing villages dot the Adriatic coast, foretelling an even simpler life as fishermen practice their ancient trade. These were much poorer areas than what we'd come to know as Italy till now and yet the unspoiled seaside and country living is richer. Their richness in the appreciation of the simple provides peace of mind, contentment with their families, faith in God and place in the world, and finding happiness in the joys of each day. *Molto Italiano.*

On our first evening out of Umbria, we land at the seaside town of Pesaro, Marche, the birthplace of Rossini. I imagine hearing Rossini's Figaro resonate through the quiet cobblestone alleys, in this humble town with shades of an era gone by. International visitors seem rare here. We came out of necessity, and are *stanca*, very tired of driving. The Hotel

Pescine which we selected on the beachfront is the bare minimum and barely open. Ray needs to summon reception. In the hotels, all windows are shaded along the beach with the heavy metal seasonal shutters soon to be lifted for the upcoming season.

Not knowing what to expect from restaurants, we venture out to find something open prior to their usual 8 PM dinner bell, or hour 20 known as the European 24-hour clock. We are pleasantly surprised by the accommodating waiter, using hand language. He understands us much better than we understood him. The shellfish he suggests are native to the area and tasted as delicious as any chic, touted restaurant to be found in Italy. The bonus is receiving two entrees at the cost of one compared to anywhere else we dined in Italy.

The following morning, we make our way south along the Adriatic, and land in a "tony" little resort called Francavilla al Mer. This gem lies just south of the larger coastal city of Pescara, kissed by the sun along the Adriatic. The Abruzzo Region is now mine to discover. Francavilla, no designer resort, has the mindset of uncomplicated living where nothing in life is too perilous. Not to worry, *il dolce far niente*, blooms like the flowers that spill out of urns and thrive with an abundance of fragrance.

Here it is, mid-May, and even in 70-degree weather, no one is out in swimwear lying on the pristine, soft, sandy expansive white beaches of Francavilla al Mer. After hibernating from winter's cold, how could this be? The beaches are at least fifty yards deep from the edge of the waves and as far as the eye could see along the coast. The sand is freshly raked, and cabanas are stationed in front of nearly every ocean-side shop.

At first, I was afraid something went terribly wrong due to the barren look. I ask a passerby why the locals are not soaking up the warm sun laden spring days. His reply, "Senora, Uno Juno", as if by religious dogma, no one suns till the first of June. This tradition is so deeply rooted, it appears to be a sin of the highest order to bare yourself in a bikini on these beaches prior to Uno Juno. "Must be considered a Mortal Sin", I say to Ray.

Hallelujah, the beach is all ours! Sun-starved and craving the wonderful warmth after an extended winter of San Francisco fog and rain, we plop our winter white bodies and dug into the sand like a couple of crabs. Our spot on the beach has its own cabana man in the shape of an Adonis. Ah, Fabio, a young muscle-bound Italian was raking and preparing the beach for the arrival of the onslaught of sun worshippers. Fabio, in his Speedo, was of perfect muscular proportion and height. With my jaw open, Ray insists on my posing with Fabio for the camera. I joyfully oblige.

Manmade jetties jut out and stretch a hundred yards across in sections, running along the coast for miles. The dark barriers appear like a string of large black pearls, perhaps strung by Poseidon himself. The waves waltz, calmly gliding in and out between the jetties.

After tumbling over the ocean floor for centuries, the rocks along the beach are polished and perfectly rounded, as if manufactured. Some are exactly circular or oval-shaped and white as snow, worth collecting and putting in a beautiful glass display jar back home. At early sunrise the next morning gemstones lie deposited on the shore from the night's waves. I scour and handpick one by one, strolling along the tide looking for the unspoiled, flawless examples of shape and color. Lodged in the sand is what appears to be a petrified shark's tooth, the prize *magnifico* piece.

My stay in Francavilla is glorious fun in the sun for two days. I am still perplexed by the bathroom shower arrangement at our deluxe boutique hotel accommodation. The showerhead fixture seems randomly placed with no enclosure and projects from the wall between the toilet and sink. A circular rod and flimsy shower curtain hang I guess, to keep the toilet sitter from getting wet. It really makes for a sandy mess after a day at the beach. Chalk it up to Italian ingenuity, simple and it works.

Today I am filled with both trepidation and exhilaration at the same time. After thirty years, I began to feel a new hunger-like instinct, to continue my magnificent obsession. I yearned to unearth and learn about my grandparents' native land. The more I find what is pleasing about all things Italian, the greater my appetite to search. All these years, I have wondered what life was left behind that inspired my great-grandparents to start anew in America. Will it be a huge disappointment, not finding any Sigismondi family members, and will the town be so rustic and poor that I realize why this lifestyle was left behind?

You see when Grandpa Dominic emigrated through Ellis Island, the Sigismondi name was chopped off to Mondi. These immigration officers were obviously in no mood for spelling. That was a mouthful, *Sigismondi.* If you want to be American you need an easier, shorter name. It was further Anglicized into Mondy with a y. I'm OK with that, however, I still like to use the "i" since most Italian words end in a vowel.

We head inland toward the Apennine Mountains to Chieti, a sizable town closer to my grandparent's home. Grandfather's name is Dominic Luigi Sigismondi and I was told by a relative's research, his hometown was "Scopoli". Grandmother's maiden name is Antonia Tate' and she was from Toricella Peligna, less than an hour from "Scopoli". Our destination is Scopoli. This was the name of the town which was given by other family members who had researched the *Mondi,* Mondy family tree back in the United States.

We wind our way past vineyards and Mediterranean-style homes of white stucco and red tile roofs. It is a climb through the hills to reach Chieti, the largest town in the province. Chieti sits high atop peaks with a panoramic overview of vineyards and farmlands. Further beyond the hills and valley, jagged mountains ascend, rising to the highest peak, The Corno Grande of The Apennine Mountains.

I get out of the car at the border of town where Chieti's large town map placard of wood stands twelve feet high. The topographic map displays the region and I look for Scopoli. Scopoli, Scopoli, no I cannot find a

Scopoli. Upon examining the map, *un poliziotto* approached us. It is Officer Umberto the chief of police donning his crisp and striking apparel, of course, designed by Giorgio Armani. He studied medicine and completed military service before he became the patron saint of designers.

I ask Umberto if he knows of Scopoli using my airport Italian and hand gesturing.

He shakes his head several times. "Scopoli? No, no, no Scopoli." He scratches his head. Our Italian friends, Giulia, and Giuseppe, back at Lake Trassemino were also stumped. "Oh! he exclaims and jumps" like an electric bolt hit him, Umberto lights up with a grand gesture of glee, and burst through his smile with "Popoli, il nome' Popoli!" Umberto is a Godsend.

Officer Umberto then explains how to get to this winding goat path of a road at a much higher elevation. Popoli is an even more remote mountaintop town than Chieti. Bravo, I congratulate Umberto for translating our misinformation and pronunciation. We had been two weeks in Italy before we figured out this puzzle of our destination; my father's family roots. I ask Umberto if he knew any Sigismondi's in the area. *"Si, Signora molto Sigismondi."* I gather, with my limited grasp of Italian, that there are at least two shops owned by Sigismondi in Chieti alone.

Umberto, with lots of arm gesturing for directions that I could roughly follow, keeps mentioning two Sigismondi cafés. He suggests we park right there on the outskirts of town as today is "*Festiva*" with no parking available. I want to roam around and see the celebration a few minutes before moving on to, ah yes, Popoli not Scopoli.

What a pleasant surprise greets us in Chieti on our unexpected arrival day, a Grand Festival for the patron saint of Abruzzo, San Giustino, is in celebration. Chieti is the provincial hill town of both high-rise contemporary buildings and ancient architecture.

Later, after research, I discover, Chieti is considered one of the most ancient Italian cities. According to a mythological legend, Chieti was founded in the 1100s BC by the Greek hero Achilles and named in honor of his mother Thetis, a sea nymph and goddess of water.

I walk around several *angoli della strada,* street corners to find the main piazza and town center. I knew something big was happening because there were swarms of priests heading in one direction. Several hundred men in their black garments with starched, upright standing tab collars with just a stiff white square in the front. As a child in Catholic school, this collar always fascinated me, like the habits or headpieces the nuns wore.

I mutter, "Holy day, it's raining priests, hallelujah, it's raining priests, A-a-amen." To our eternal gratefulness it was a Holy Day, where the Cathedral held its annual festivities for the patron saint San Giustino. A church can be named a Cathedral only if it is deemed the most important church of the bishop's diocese and holds his throne. Once we reach the piazza, with the Cathedral in sight, priests are pattering up the steps last minute to their private Mass celebration. What a vision to behold.

The parade and festival are an incredible display of pride, pomp, and circumstance. Speaking of circumstance, I knew it was Divine Intervention meant for our arrival since we came upon this annual celebration completely unaware. My unplanned timing is serendipity. The entire town of Chieti is involved in one way or another. So much piety in one place makes me feel spiritual and vulnerable, yet ecstatic at the same time. It brought this former Catholic schoolgirl to her knees in prayer.

I pray inside the Cathedral before the priest's Mass was to begin and I implore God to help me find my family tree. "Trust in the Lord" when it hit me, "go to the phone book." They still had them. Nothing divine or difficult about it. That's it, I thought, certainly there's no more than a few Sigismondi's in town and they could help me associate and connect our family. We then plopped outside on the steps and curiously watched the bustle of activity in preparation for the parade in the piazza below. Like an aberration in time, on the side of the church was a carnival ride, a traveling carnival octopus, appearing completely out of place around ancient structures.

I thumb through the phonebook to the S section. Mama Mia, my ingenious idea was thwarted by a listing of eight plus pages of Sigismondi's, numbering in the hundreds. I thought about going to city hall, but with limited time and grasp of Italian, and being the only Americans in town, and no one speaking English, I realize I need another trip to further my search. Besides, here in Italy, if they like you, most warmhearted Italians welcome you into their home as if you were family, particularly if you're of Italian blood.

I stroll further through town on the main street and hear a marching band and the sound of trumpets comes marching past us. A parade in military fashion with men of all ages dressed alike, they wear navy jackets, dark slacks, crisp white shirts, and silk burgundy ties. The horn section has a cool big band swing beat number going. The faces of the marching musicians beam, as they march erect with a spark of pride in their stride. The horns and drums resound off buildings, as the marching band struts down the promenade. What a joy for musicians and music lovers alike!

Under the arches of porticos, merchandise of all kinds, including arts and crafts are on display for sale. This is my first shopping experience under the portal halls and gives my purchase symbolic significance to an era of shopping that has existed here for centuries. Leather goods of shoes, purses, wallets, belts, etc. line the sidewalks. A beautiful hand-woven brown belt for Ray is my first purchase and a natural color leather shoulder bag is my purse of choice.

On the major promenade, I come upon my first ancestral family find at a *bella* Café *Impero,* Emperor, owned by a Sigismondi. *Mio Nonno*, my grandfather's last name was written in cursive on the sign above the café portal. The café in typical Italian order, housed nothing less than a deli, coffee, gelato, a bar and umbrella covered tables that stretched outside to the lane. As I order my gelato, I ask the server if the owner Sigismondi is in. I say, "I am visiting from California and *mio padre's famiglia il nome et Sigismondi,* my father's family name is Dominic Sigismondi."

Bisnonno, Grandpa Dominic Sigismondi

There was a flurry to the door. A patron or owner's friend, without a word, hurried outside to retrieve Luigi Sigismondi, the owner. The clerk tried to explain to me his sudden departure in seeking Luigi. He arrived in a minute, eager to greet me and after a few minutes of hand language translation, we hugged and paused for a photograph. After many years of anticipation and all the hours focused on the moment of meeting family in Italy has arrived. Since we are unable to communicate but a few words, I have no way of interpreting his lineage. I smile, noticing his features and thinking, a distant cousin, no doubt and gratifying to finally absorb the surroundings of my ancestry.

I venture further around the piazza and within a few blocks, happen upon another namesake shop of Sigismondi. This little family store carried toiletry items, postage, lottery, various sundries and even horse betting.

Goods were stacked to the ceiling, which took serious perusing to find items on your own. The clerk was very busy with lottery ticketing, so as not to interrupt, I merely stepped back and laughed about the horse betting. There were three clerks in a small bedroom size shop and with more than two customers, movement was a challenge.

I had expected more ability to connect and knew not what to expect. Sadly, I later find out that Chieti had been one of the worst World War II prison encampments for officers. Many were later tried for war crimes. Now it makes sense as to why some of the more modern high-rise buildings of fifties-sixties architecture were prominent in this town of rebuilding from the war.

Since the morning had escaped us and the afternoon was running short, it was time to head to Popoli. On our way to Popoli we are side-tracked, take a wrong turn, and are lost. While Ray gasses up the Fiat, I approach a scraggly unshaven man at the gas station who appears to be herding sheep that day. I ask for our way to Popoli. He proceeds to explain in Italian, *"Prendere Sinistro..., un altra sinistro,l'ovest...et a destra..."* all the while arms flapping, fingers pointing and loud tones that barely make sense in my abbreviated understanding. I got "turn left, blah, blah, blah, another left, blah, blah, blah, head west and then right..."

When the shepherd was gesturing, along comes a priest on a bicycle with his black garments blowing. The priest or Don overheard the poor man's directions. The priest of saving grace, who spoke a bit of English, made more sense in our getting back on track. "*Grazie Padre*." The unshaven shepherd hits his head with the butt of his hand in exasperation and proceeds to argue with the priest, arms flailing as we drive off.

Popoli at Last

Winding up the mountains on the goat hill roads of The Appenine Mountains in Abruzzo, our journey's destination lies in the southeast central region of Italy. I discover the natural wonders of my grandparents' homeland. Bordered on the east by the Adriatic Sea and The Parco Nazionale d'Abruzzo on the West. The park is the largest and one of the best-preserved national forests in Europe. Harbored within are the wildlife of deer, foxes, and wolves.

Some of my family roots are in The Abruzzo Region, due east of Roma. Abruzzo beckons where simpler people exist, living off the land. *La dolce vita* reigns here in the day-to-day village life and continues here unlike anywhere in the United States today. Abruzzo residents are genuine and have the time to engage in chance meetings and surprise visits. For some, their day is what the day brings them.

How can one not love Italy when at least a region or two or three of the twenty regions have such diversity in lifestyle and geography, perhaps as different as a New York City broker and a Nebraska farmer. I believe the closely knit trust in a community was an era lost around the 1960s in the United States. But here in the tightly knit mountain villages where generations continue to reside, resident Italians have the comfort and luxury of greeting each other favorably day to day, knowing their neighbors as lifetime friends or adversaries. At least they know their adversary.

Abruzzo is dotted with small villages throughout. I find solace here where the two most magnificent natural wonders of *montagne,* mountain, *mare*, and sea surround the region.

Near the end of my Italian journey, I finally discover one branch of the family tree, the town of my grandfather's childhood. He died before I was born in New York and one of the links I needed to connect with him had been born here. A small village asleep amidst the hot springs. *Popoli,* the village of my heritage, had evaded me and had barely awakened for my arrival.

Popoli is a town situated amidst *terme* hot springs. It hits me like a blast from the past or *mai visto,* certain this was the reason my father was drawn to Glenwood Springs, Colorado one of the world's largest hot springs pools and located in the Rocky Mountains of Colorado.

Glenwood Springs, near Aspen, is just a few hours from our Denver home. Every summer we'd pack six or seven siblings in the car with a little trailer in tow, and the treacherous climb over Loveland Pass. This was before the Eisenhower Tunnel cut through the mountain pass.

We'd invade this "world's largest hot springs pool" and swim for days on end unattended in our gigantic orange life preservers. Mom put those blazing orange life preservers on all seven of us kids and let us loose the rest of the day. You floated like the ocean's salt water in this mineral pool, so no worries. These were the happiest days of my childhood with the ability to escape parental control, taking slick rides down the slides with a crash, spray, and gulp of water, jumping off diving boards, and riding a merry-go-round that spun bodies flying off into the water. Add to this, fountains in the middle of the pool. And you have our version of Disneyland and Water world.

As we twisted and turned speedily up the one-lane road, I felt the pull of the curvy road and the familiar smell of rotten eggs lingering, which hot springs emit. Glenwood Springs, Colorado had the same smell of sulfur. A rush of emotion washes over me as a lump swell in my throat and I fight back tears, not from the foul odor, but from a memory flash that Dad never got the chance to visit Popoli or Italy for that matter.

Dad, Vincent Dominick Mondi, and Mom, Madeline, had their tickets and passport in hand, ready to meet me in Rome. A mild stroke a few months prior prevented Dad from traveling. He was in his late seventies and by doctor's advice he canceled. I believe the doctor's advice was a death sentence to his spirit: by focusing on the chance of "What if you have a stroke and die over there?" I know visiting his homeland in Italy would have been a newly discovered awakening and added years to his life. Papa Vicenzo is riding with me in spirit today.

The smell of sulfur quickly dissipates, as our hunger cries out, and behold a little restaurant we spot by the road on the outskirts of town. This fascinating trattoria was in a cavern or subterranean hollow. The restaurant had arched groin ceilings and two levels of seating. The antipasto that arrived on its own reminded me exactly of what we grew up with as my dad's favorite. Marinated sweet peppers, celery, and carrots were served with salami. Olive oil and vinegar dressing accompanied these simple ingredients. I gorged down a classic spaghetti dish and house *vino Rosso* because the anticipation of finally arriving and finding our way to the Popoli Piazza is a cause for celebration. We relished the simple local ingredients and hurried along to the piazza.

In case you're seeing a pattern here, yes, it is the piazza of every town large or small that is the pulse and heartbeat of the community. The piazza is where I sit to absorb the local culture and fare. *Festivas,* festivals, to honor one of a bazillion saints across Italy, spring up regularly in the piazzas. Entering Popoli, the fresh welcome fragrance of wisteria lingers and dashes the sulfur away. The block square piazza has a giant pergola covered with plentiful vines of lavender wisteria. These purplish blooms are so dense they create a tunnel inside the pergola arches where only patches of sunlight sneak through.

The town is nearly vacant, and Ray stops me to take a photo while I peer under the vines in this refreshingly untainted-by-tourists town. The village has its share of deteriorated buildings and is so remote, the feeling of being an anomaly dawned on me. We were being watched as a spectacle, as we simply take photos in the middle of the piazza under the giant pergola with draping wisteria.

I feel the stare of eyeballs and noticed four idle old men positioned on a bench across the street. Their appearance is a throwback to another era in the 1940s. They enjoy this simple manner of life passing the time idly away, *il dolce far niente.* This is particularly common in the sunset years as a privilege of senior passage.

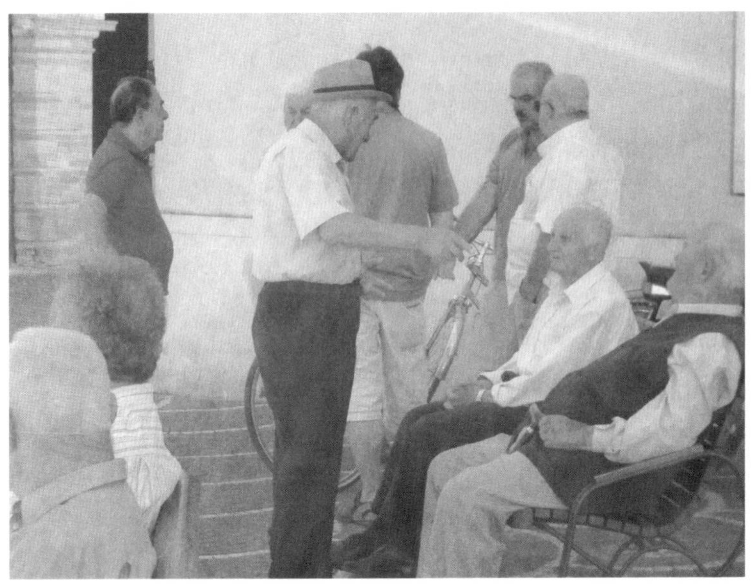

Across the street from the piazza, sit three men who wore their age, seventies I'd say, on a newly painted, bright green bench. A fourth man stood with the bench fully occupied. They were poised in front of a building, two stories high and painted in pastel pink. The standing man wears a fedora and holds his chin as if to discern from what planet we had landed. We'll call him Luigi, the talker and most definitely the fashionista of the four. He holds his hand over his mouth, "Who are those aliens?" Luigi wears a crisp collared shirt as do the others, and two even have cuffs for their casual sit on the bench this afternoon-one bald, one receding hairline with white hair in a crisp white shirt. The man sitting on the right end of the bench donned a sweater vest. One sits erect, and stares directly at my camera as if posing. A standing man nearby with a bicycle, scratches his chin, and looks over to a restaurant front.

Il quattro, the four partakers of *far niente*, are established members of the community. I imagine they spend every day talking in the piazza as a favorite pastime, how and where their imaginations allow them. They hold dear one another's presence even with uneventful purpose.

Perhaps some days were spent playing chess or bocce ball. Bocce ball is a favorite game like lawn bowling of Italy. I had a crash course on bocce ball in Sonoma County one morning after playing tennis in Gorky Park in the town of Healdsburg, California where I resided. Anthony, *Antonio* Lucca from Lucca, Italy introduced me to the basics of the game. Antonio was the keeper of the court. Every morning he came and raked the dirt for practice.

Reminiscing now about my grandparents, Nicola, *bisnonno* my great grandfather, bravely crossed the Atlantic to the United States in search of the golden opportunities America boasted. Nicola was 28 years old when freedom and fortune most certainly allured him to leave a wife and three young children behind until he could make a way for his family. His wife, Maria obviously heard opportunity knocking and departed later that year from Italy on New Year's Eve, 1897 from the port of Naples.

Bisnonna Maria boldly boards the ship Victoria with their three young children in tow. Vincenzo age five, Antonia age two and Erminica, five months. In Maria's pocket is the grand sum of eight dollars for the long, arduous ocean crossing. Maria Piccoli *Teti,* Tate lands on Ellis Island twenty-three days later with the three little ones and continues her journey to this bold change of life.

Today as I watch a mother boarding a Trans-Atlantic flight with three little ones, I think of the inexhaustible task such a journey demands even with all the modern accommodations. I can't imagine the strength and sustenance summoned for this ocean journey from Naples, crossing the Atlantic, accomplished by my great grandmother Maria Piccoli with my Grandmother Antonia then age 2, and her two young siblings.

Grandma, Nonna Antonia, set foot on the land of the free and the home of the brave as a babe, unaware of how her life was to transform from the mountains of central Italy. As a woman standing five foot nothing, Antonia with determination and an intense demeanor bore 13 children in New York and Pennsylvania. Mama Mia! Her parents were Nicola *Teti*, anglicized to Tate, and Maria *Piccoli* Tate born in Toricella Peligna, Abruzzo, Italy in 1869 and 1870.

It is too late in the day to drive to the next destination of Toricella Peligna, and we don't know exactly how to get there, so it is decided that Peligna will have to loom in my imagination. We must push on to a road that leads to Rome.

Later back home in Healdsburg, I came to realize that my visit to Abruzzo coincided or marked exactly with the one hundred-one years since the death of my *bisnonno* Great Grandfather, Niccolo Piccoli in Toricella Peligna. Peligna is the birthplace of Niccolo and grandma, his daughter, Antonia. Antonia came to America at a tender three years of age with her mother, Maria, my great Grandmother.

I wanted to savor the flavor of Popoli, Abruzzo. Alas, we were left with only a few short hours to linger among the sights and smells. Devoted to simple mountain village living with small family shops, and a refreshing love for life, generations have sprung from this village of Popoli. There is nothing astonishing about this little village, however, it now looms large in the meaning and discovery of my family tree, Sigismondi.

It's simply extraordinary when compared to our modern, detailed lives back home. Firmly rooted in a region dense with forests, Abruzzo is remarkably the largest forested area in all of Italy. The golden eagle soars and dives through the trees with a kee-aar screech resounding over the Apennine mountains as an everlasting impression of Spring.

Chapter 3

Living Italian at Lago, Lake Trasimeno, Umbria

After a spine-tingling drive through the streets of Roma and heading a few hours north outside the bustling city, the peaceful panoramic view of *Lago*, Lake Trasimeno is more *magnifico* than I imagined. Villa Liliana is surrounded by rolling, wavelike hills which my husband Ray and I called home for two weeks, and it may as well have been two years with the comfort and generosity extended by owners Giuseppe and Giulia.

We arrive in Umbria following several monumental days around the Vatican where everything was blessed by Spring. *La Primavera* blooms with freshness in the air. On entering the grounds leading up to Villa Liliana, we hadn't a clue as to the daily rigor and hairpin climb required. The salutes of cypress, and swaying poppies made for a glorious welcome.

The wide dirt and gravel entry road is framed by a line of Italian Cypress thirty feet high and half mile long. The rows of cypress stand erect, as if to serve a formal welcome greeting. The regal cypress with their well-shaped posture, gives me a feeling of grandness at first sight. They rarely need trimming to maintain shape. "Hello ever standing, vigilant soldier, oh Italian Cypress, thank you for the salute" I proclaim. Salute indeed.

Intuitively, learning later that cypress trees were planted across Italy in honor of fallen soldiers during World War II.

Turning and winding up the climbing dirt road, as the curves pull, the ascent is a bumpy thirteen hairpin turns of switchback after switch-back. No chance for a quick espresso into town or a forgotten toothbrush trip. We had ourselves committed for the day once setting out or returning to the villa on this serpentine road. We drive past fields of blooming red poppies stretched like a delicate, uneven red carpet. Then we pass orchards of unruly, overgrown olive trees with their silver-grey leaves reflecting light and the branches twisting and turning skyward to greet the sun. A pan-orama that exacts its price in driving, is well worth the reward.

Our villa selection was made easy, because of its convenient location to Perugia and Florence, as well as towns we wished to visit in both Tuscany and Umbria. My Dad, Vincent Dominick suggested his family came from the Perugia area in Umbria which became my main quest. Umbria is known as the "Green Heart of Italy." The fields of olive trees and grape-vines weave like a wild patchwork quilt. I count over ten shades of green - from yellow-green chartreuse to dark olive forest green and everything in between. The name Umbria is perfectly suitable, since *ombra* means shade, in a land sharing many shades of green. Splendor in the hills, oh trodden turf of ancient times, grows fresh in April as if blooming for the first time to spread out before us.

Village towers in Umbria erupt at the tops of hillsides like lava spew-ing up and out of Mt. Vesuvius in Pompeii. Medieval fortresses still stand intact from where they were originally built. Remnants of ancient civiliza-tion coexist with modern buildings without pause. Villagers scurry to the market for contemporary conveniences, a farmer's market for local fresh produce. Vegetables and fruit are precisely displayed like jewels under a showcase at Tiffany's.

Bask in the sweetness of doing nothing, *il dolce far niente*. Many vil-lages are surrounded by layers of three walls built from three eras - Etruscan,

Roman, and Renaissance. Some walls stand with little damage while others crumble to skeletal form with age. Giuseppe explained to us that Umbria is named after the Umbra settling in 6 BC -- Etruscans followed alongside the Umbrians.

On my third venture to Italy, traveling past Tuscany and across the Umbrian border, my two weeks stay at the villa, provided my first ever, reinvigorating experience in the countryside, something I had not the luxury to indulge in before. Umbria is subdued and mysterious and less crowded with tourists, unlike Tuscany. Umbria is a central target in the boot of Italy, from north, south, east, or west, and more landlocked than any region.

Ray joined me in the selection of Villa Liliana from months earlier back home. Something about this property struck a chord after thumbing through many pages of properties. Relaxing in the serenity overlooking *Lago*, Lake Trasimeno, our instincts about the area were everything I hoped for and more. As we ventured through hills rich in history, the crisp and unhurried surroundings forced a focus on nature and ancient buildings both crumbled and modernly refurbished. I became mesmerized by the sensation of ages never seen or experienced. The surrounding towns of Assisi, Perugia, Orvieto, and Deruta are desired destinations as each village seduces with its own distinct religious history, scenery, family traditions, and artisans.

The view of Lake Trasimeno conjures images of the battle spot where Hannibal conquered the Romans, in the 200s BC. Hannibal left Carthage, originating from Tunisia, Africa, and crossed the Mediterranean, landing in Spain, and across Gaul or France with his mighty army. They thundered over the Alps, with his herd of elephants, and into Italy. The elephants were bound by chains and mini fortresses atop their backs, carrying several soldiers at a time. Imagine the sight and sounds of elephants trumpeting and pounding over the rugged Alps from Spain to Italy, when my only other memory of elephants is Dumbo or the zoo. Elephants amidst the battle at Hannibal's Point contributed to a Roman defeat around the lake. He is known as among the greatest military strategists alongside Alexander the Great and Julius Caesar.

Hannibal's conquest was short-lived, however, because the Romans readily defeated Hannibal into submission a few months later. As I look over the lay of the land, soaked in history, it is humbling to fathom this monumental event now 2,200 years later. I have arrived from a country established just over 200 years ago.

Vineyards lined on the hill where twisted, thickened dark vines (think of bare trees at Halloween-like goons) suddenly open their sprouts of blooming green leaves in spring. If you've ever witnessed grapevines in the winter, you'd swear they were dead with their barren, gnarly limbs. Life appears miraculously at the first sign of spring with little green sprouts erupting from these lifeless-looking limbs of burnt umber. Vines grow into Sangiovese grapes so famous to the Tuscan/Umbrian Wine Regions for Chianti.

Chianti *vino* is medium-bodied and red, full of blackberry, plum, and cherry flavors. The gastronomic variety in each region has evolved into luscious flavors and cuisines. Row after row of vines stretches across vine-yards, as we drive by, on finely groomed terraces. They begin as grapes the size of pinhead bundles every spring, on the landscape that has produced grapes for centuries. The blooms of April produce bundles of succulent grapes six months later in October's harvest.

Viticulture was also introduced in Sonoma California in the late 1800s just a mile up from my first home in Healdsburg, California. Our own introduction to vineyards began with terracing several rows of merlot grapes in our backyard acre developing into a little boutique vineyard two years later producing 150 bottles. My full attention is given to the labor and beauty of viticulture. I wore two hats back home in San Francisco: city girl teaching ballet and farm girl, cultivating and harvesting grapes with my straw hat and grapevine cutters.

The meticulous Italian terracing was like none other I've seen, even while living in Sonoma County, the heart of California wine country. The giant spread and quantity of vines in their perfect lines give way to designs of optical illusion.

Back in Umbria, we drive in our little Fiat, passing through a herd of about forty sheep bleating in the warmth of the sun, so thick with wool they could scarcely take a worthwhile step. "Ba-a-ah, Ba-a-a-ah, look at you hapless creatures eating and wandering, wandering, and eating over your pasture, soon to be brought to the shearing. "Thanks for the fine Italian merino wool sweaters I love wearing on my back," I shout out, "You poor sheep." The shepherd who drives up in his four-wheeler assures me they feel better after the shearing. "They're ready to receive the summer's sun," Giulio said.

We venture past a dozen ancient villas crumbling and distressed, all with very few signs of life when I started wondering what an undertaking villa restoration would mean. Those that inhabited these ancient dwellings intermingled with life on the land, sustenance known today as "farm to table." There is a higher intelligence to a full life with all its inherent simple yet sometimes backbreaking duties and the rhythm of a natural passing of time immersed in nature.

A simpler life is lost in the fast lane, info-tech, quick to boredom world of ours in America. Sitting here with a computer would feel like an intrusion of sorts yet Italians blend modern conveniences with ease. It was not mine to worry about the extra passing of time getting to and from our villa because we are witness to life and cultivation in Umbria as it has been lived for centuries.

Our setting on the hillside makes the township of Passignano from atop Villa Liliana appear as a brush of red-tiled roofs. Bricks of terracotta painted the village in one color from the distance. The whole town was dwarfed from this vantage point and could be covered by the spread of my hand stretched out in front of me.

Passignano feels casual, quaint, and lovely on the lakefront, housing residents of the simpler life. We found an artisan craftsman displaying fine art ceramics known as Majolica for sale outside, propped randomly on chairs and tables like a spontaneous garage sale. The Italian ceramics of Majolica became popular with nobility in the Renaissance and newer copies are made with a white base glaze.

The gracious and warmhearted owners of Villa Liliana, Giuseppe, and Giulia made our stay enchanting. They truly are exuberant in Italian spirit and exemplify hospitality, whether hosting for resident occupants, dinner, or travel as they share their life's adventures.

Trapolina is their wire-haired dachshund who ran like a jackrabbit toward the car as we drove up, her low grounded legs spurred with unbelievable speed and agility. I'd never seen this strange looking breed of dog before and told Ray, "She looks part muskrat, part dachshund." We feared her little legs would give out running near the tires. She became our houseguest and the most memorable of all friend's dogs. She filled a void in missing my beloved West Highland Terrier, Ziggy. He was my little gentleman and shadow of ten years waiting back home.

The first morning we arose, Trapolina's long snout and expressive hazel eyes sat at our doorstep. We welcomed her in for a few nibbles of breakfast. Trapolina's, human-like, penetrating hazel eyes inspired immediate bonding as if she were our own.

Giuseppe is out on the lawn, perched on his mower with the loud puttering engine, grooming the lawn and landscaping around the pool. The fresh morning air in the countryside is intoxicating. He and Giulia are very ambitious renovators working at a steadfast pace on the long-neglected estate. Giulia plants rosemary herbs and delicate blue flowers next to the stacked stone, beautifying the already captivating grounds.

As we stand on the grassy terrace, out of the blue I hear a small plane engine buzzing, dipping, and diving. The sound changes octaves in its descent. I was afraid we might have to hit the ground flat as the pilot dive bombs right over our villa towards us. He plateaus at the last second to come within fifty feet of our rooftop. Twice he pulled this daring stunt just in case we missed the first one or weren't impressed enough as the engine roared past uncomfortably close.

Giulia rushes over to inform us, "This is our pilot friend in the air show." "I might have guessed based on that familiarizing gesture swooping down," I replied. She explains they are helping host a small airplane show the same weekend we arrive in Castiglione al Mer, a village on the other side of the Lake. Neither Giulia nor Giuseppe had any desire ever to fly. I found out why toward the end of our stay when we invited them to come to visit us in California.

Giulia and Giuseppe's home was approximately thirty yards from our villa. Giulia's art studio is set right above our villa on the second floor. Some days she'd walk up the cement stairs to her little studio with an extraordinarily large window, then stand to take in the expansive view overlooking hillside and lake. She painted lively watercolor brush strokes of the lake view spread out before her. Painting for many Italians is second nature.

One evening after joining in Giulia's authentic local Umbrian cuisine, she led us to her collection of paintings in the art studio. She pulls out several paintings, both landscape and modern, neatly tucked in art file drawers. Her talent with watercolors is so apparent that I was immediately drawn to a couple of the panoramic scenes. She also shared a more modern style of reflective underwater scenes with the rocks outlined on the lake's outline from her summer memories of snorkeling around the Ionian islands of Greece.

The watercolors I select as choices are a view from our Villa Liliana and the grounds at Hannibal's Point surrounding Lake Trasimeno. I carry the views of Lake Trasimeno and the villa in packed suitcases and bring them back to our condo which I called a "land yacht" in Sausalito. Jumping into those paintings next to my desk from time to time helps me relive the magic, like Alice through the looking glass.

Giulia loved tending to her garden during our visit. She shared her plans with Giuseppe on continuing the renovation of this once abandoned home and guesthouse. I shared in that love back home and developed a fondness for Giulia since she was always quick with assistance, gracious and sensitive--true to Italian form. I was simply the guest at her villa, and she welcomed us royally. She and Giuseppe invited us to dinner more than once.

The patio deck from our villa was framed by a pergola, an arbor entwined with a grapevine. Many terracotta pots bordered the stone stack deck that climbed five steps up from the grassy terrace. These are familiar features in Italian gardens. Here is our glory view spanning as far across the lake and hillside, as the eye could see.

The second evening at Lake Trasimeno we take our rental wagon, which is good to carry luggage for four, down thirteen hairpin turns to stock up on groceries and wine for our weeklong visit. I notice a black and white bird just ahead of the car, weaving in and out of a row of tall Italian cypress trees like a thread through the fabric. I'm fascinated by the stature of the trees and the direction the bird seems to be leading on our way down the long road toward Lake Trasimeno.

On entering the market, we peruse the cramped aisles and marvel at the differences in goods, wondering what is contained within bags and boxes. The deli display contained cheese wheels of asiago and pecorino, buffalo mozzarella, ricotta, and mascarpone. The difference is curing time compared to America, their aging process is years - cured meats such as salami sausages, capicola, and prosciutto. After an hour of figuring out the merchandise and translating with the butcher, we loaded the back of the wagon to the hilt with enough food for weeks.

The evening descended quickly to dark by the time we departed the market. On the drive back up the serpentine hill, we bounce through a pothole with a giant thud that seemed to swallow the front of the car. We sat stunned with our heavy load of groceries in the back of the wagon.

Ray piles out of the car as I jump behind the wheel and await the sudden shout and prompt to "Gun it!" After rocking the car forcefully to push out of the hole, we jump back in. Ray gets behind the wheel again. An immediate sound from underneath the car began with a dragging noise below. I shout out, "I sure hope we make it to the top." The annoying sound, up and around another two hairpin turns, halts. Kaput! The car dies. In the light of the full moon, after piling out of the car again, we could see a leaky trail of black oil on the road behind us.

So... we each grab a grocery sack or two and start our trek. Thank God for *la luna,* the full moon. We laugh and joke about our folly. I start singing Dean Martin's "When the moon hits'a you eyes like a big pizza pie, that's Amore." After trudging halfway up the hill toward our villa, I felt a pounding of the earth that stopped my heart, and we heard a stomping rustle behind the bushes.

An attack of fear and frozen feet hit me. I could feel the rumbling movement on the ground yet could not see over the brush on the moonlit hill to know what beasts were standing by. Either one enormous animal or a herd of them was next to us, yet invisible. Within seconds it occurred to me, the pounding hoofs against the earth that we awakened a herd of sheep. They were as alarmed of us, as we were of them. In the presence of their wooly animal smell and the rustling with the kicked-up dust spread through the air, we chuckle and continue walking a half mile up to the villa with our load of groceries and vino.

Again, we break out singing Dean Martin style, "When 'a the moon hits you eyes, like a big pizza pie, that's Amore." After a long day behind us, we finally make it home for unpacking groceries, and serve up a nice 'a spaghetti dinner with a long day behind us and a very peaceful setting to get recharging sleep that night.

Ray calls the rental car agency the next day to hear that it is a Holy Day weekend, which means another few days before anyone is working to switch out cars near Siena. Giulia and Giuseppe are so kindhearted that

Giulia offers, "You can use my car the next couple of days." Her little Fiat Punto looked so compact yet these Italians have mastered maximizing interior space, and we were amazed at the comfort.

The following day, billowy grey-green clouds hang over the hills surrounding the lake. The clouds are suspended at the hilltops as if a force of nature is blowing them back and holding them in place so as not to cast a shadow over the lake and maintain sparkling, green water. On the other side of the lake lies Casteliogne del Mer, the site of the airshow which we visit later in the week. A charming little village with a welcoming fountain piazza.

I find a food shop selling wild boar sausage with a boar's head mounted like a trophy above the entry of the market. Dark wood shelves displayed cheeses, olives, crackers, and seasonings. I purchased a jar of Italian Seasonings native to the region of Umbria for marinara sauce. Giulia mentioned these spices. The sprinkling of *pepperoncino*, crushed chili peppers, and seeds, is popular in Umbria, and used for tomato sauce with a zing.

Worth their taste in gold, and precious to this region are the *tartufo,* black truffles, *nero* which are rare. This is a good thing because they're pricey. Just a hint of truffle in a sauce or dusting gives a distinctively rich, biting flavor to savor. These considered jewels are unearthed by the pigs or dogs trained to snort and dig rigorously for them in the dark damp soils of spring or fall. People pay to go out with the pigs and find them digging for these treasures. The truffle farmers keep their locations top secret. A rich hint of truffle shavings with olive oil and parmesan cheese over pasta is heaven to taste and one of my treasured favorites.

The next day Giuseppe and Giulia prepare a table outside for their Sunday family feast of May, gathering on the grassy terrace between their villa and our guest villa. I ask Giulia about the darting black and white birds that lead our way ahead of the car weaving along the cypress tree-lined road. She mentioned, "They originate from Africa," with a name

I could not decipher any better than the "Go Away" bird, in her Italian accent. Once again Giulia offers the ultimate Italian welcome by inviting us along with British and Italian friends and family members to join in their family feast.

The setting gave me reminders of my own family meals every Sunday with the long table for seven children. Aunts and Uncles or friends of the family were always joining in. Like when my dad invited home the stray airmen from his work at Lowry Air Force Base in Denver dying for a home meal. "Flyboys" we called them in the Air Force.

Matteo, Giulia's brother, age 40, with dark and rugged good looks, talks to Ray and proudly boasts, "I've never been to Rome." Ray asks, "Why not?" in disbelief. "Rome is just a few hours' drive." Matteo says, "I prefer Turkey whose Roman ruins are much more intact, less crowded, and commercial." Ray and I look at each other and try not to laugh at the reasoning.

Obviously, the frequent pot smoking curbed his ambition.

We later decided to ferry across Lake Trasimeno to the little island in the middle, Isola Maggiore, where a giant castle stood. It was a religious holiday weekend, for St. Francis of Assisi, which can last up to five days. Some from nearby Florence, were taking their vacation in the countryside.

Women line up to board the ferry on dirt paths in stiletto heels and dresses as if going to the theater in Florence. What a sight for a truly casual outing with a smirk of impropriety. I also admire the women who dress so-o-o like women, spilling over in femininity. The young machismo is smooching and hugging their *bella* beauties. Once aboard, with a kiss, kiss here, and a wraparound hug there, *amore'* is in the air.

Speaking of holidays, I decided to adopt the vacation habits of Western European countries, particularly Italy. In total, upwards of over 40 vacation days a year are granted to Italians. They take the lead in Europe. Weekend holidays run at least four to five days, a fine example that their time is not as equated with money.

A Pilgrimage to Assisi

Our first day trip from Villa Liliana to Assisi is in the Province of Perugia. For many years, I believed my ancestry lay mainly in Perugia. The medieval town of Assisi is so rich in religious spirit and monuments that peace and meditation permeate the air. The line of traffic from the highway to the top of the hill town says this peace must come to a halt since a giant pilgrimage is in progress. We decide to return in a few days, but then…

The *carabinieri,* who also patrol the military, sit at the base of the ramp, and decide to pull us over as suspects. I'd never witnessed a policeman yielding a semiautomatic weapon, so I thought they were looking for big trouble and a major crime. The two handsome *carabinieri* were intensely focused at first, but after examining Ray's California driver's license, they beam a smile, saying "Americano", and granting us mercy to continue our journey with directions back to the villa.

Saint Francis is my favorite patron saint as the lover of nature and animals. He is the patron saint of Italy, and it appears he is everyone's favorite in Italy for pilgrimage on our May Day, weekend visit. He had an unprecedented following due to his charisma and humility. Born into wealth he chose poverty. More admirable than being poor since it is extremely difficult to part with our comforts. St. Francis made Assisi the founding place of the Franciscan religious order of Friars and Roman Catholic priests.

Frescoes of St. Francis' on the chapel walls depict the virtues of faith, hope, and charity. I make a mental note that I need to do more for the needy back home. St. Francis of Assisi fostered one of the most recognized and recited prayers in the Catholic Faith and is one of my favorites:

Lord make me an instrument of your peace.

Where there is hatred let me sow love,

Where there is injury, pardon

Where there is doubt, faith

Where there is despair, hope

Where there is darkness, light

O Divine Master, grant that I may not so much seek to be consoled, as to console,

To be understood, as to understand, to be loved as to love. For it is in giving that we receive, it is in pardoning that we are pardoned, and it is in dying that we are born to eternal life.

The St. Francis peace prayer is on the holy card distributed at my father's funeral, Vincent Dominick Mondy, on October 16, 2002.

On our return to Assisi, Friars are roaming all over the Basilica grounds, courtyard, and behind the display of religious artifacts for sale. They are cloaked in brown robes with large, rounded collars, some cinched at the waist with a rope and a rosary. I thought these outfits from ages ago were no longer worn. It is a part of their tradition that keeps them grounded in the longevity of their faith. I bought rustic wooden rosaries, medals, and gold leaf plaques or icons of St. Francis. We had them blessed by one of the Franciscan Friars standing in the entry of the chapel. Without a doubt, I felt closer to grace and God in the presence of such religious history.

One of Italy's foremost monuments, The Basilica of St. Francis, has three levels with both an upper and lower cathedral, capturing both Gothic and Renaissance architecture. There is a distinct atmosphere and presence of peace here. The frescoed walls are beautifully restored from the earthquake of 1997, just a few years prior. In the upper chapel, Martini created both the frescoes and stained glass. The lower chapel holds panels on the Life of St. Francis by Giotto. Indescribably *bella*, beautiful and breathtaking to absorb in one afternoon. Giotto had tremendous influence as a painter of his time. St. Francis lies below the lower chapel in a crypt.

Calendimaggio, May 1, our May Day is the religious celebration in the town of Assisi where crimson and navy banners are draped like window valances from stone building to building and wrapped around pillars. Green garlands strung with gold bulbs and ribbon hang between columns to ornament the parade celebration as if it were Christmas. I heard that the evening we missed over the weekend with the breakdown of our car, there was a competition of love songs where sections of the city compete with one another. I can hear the melodies ringing and singing through the columns.

We are *fame,* famished after climbing countless stone stairs, wandering through alleys of a quaint town that embraces you in its arms, near the comfort only a mother can give. The church grounds cover acres. For lunch we meander to the end of a long, winding, quiet alleyway and discover a simple café in a reception hall full of locals. I order my favorite dish of linguine with *tartufo*, truffles, in a creamy sauce that melts in my mouth with their bold, distinguished flavor.

After lunch, we continue down the *vicolo,* alley and find an alleyway that was so narrow Ray stretches his arms across and touches either side of the walls and can't even extend his arms having to bend his elbows. He plays Hercules flexing and acting as if he were holding the walls apart, preventing them from closing in. An overall image of the town is framed in my mind with attractive floral clay urns accenting the edge of the stairway, facing the cupolas or church towers that are Assisi.

Passing an art shop, etchings are displayed with many versions of Assisi's turning lanes and cobbled alleyways. Black block ink prints texture and accentuate the bricks and stones. I am drawn to an etching print, which shows a curved alley leading to the St. Francis Basilica and Cupola.

Through St. Francis, I derive the genteel nature in one of God's favored sons. While winding up our journey I am humbly reminded by the words of St. Francis, my inability to control destiny. "What are we but the jesters of God?"

If you know Italian drivers, speeding is an essential survival skill on the road. I bumped Ray's thigh and raised an eyebrow saying, "I must make a bathroom stop." We agree at the AutoGrill rest stop, to insist we go back to the villa, pronto.

The next morning back at Villa Liliana, we enjoy breakfast out on the terrace in the sun's warmth with our expansive lake view, and we have a little visitor. Seated on the long bench and table, I notice a black snake curled up next to one of the large terracotta pots. I elbow Ray, thinking the little demon is probably a garden variety, but still, I do not like snakes. My four brothers terrorized me with their pet bull snake and garter snakes collected from creeks in the neighborhood when we were kids.

Ray jumps up and shouts "I think that's a baby viper!" Oh Joy, the poisonous viper must have come out of winter's nesting to sun himself on the stacked stones of the terrace. Ray runs up to Giuseppe and Giulia's home and she came back wielding a shovel. Giulia pounded the shovel end time and time again right over the snake's head and cut it off in a ritual way of killing, perhaps to keep the devil from returning. Execution is handily accomplished. She examined the stone pile and suggested we continue to "keep an eye out". I guess we wi-i-i-l-l-l.

Later that afternoon as we return from sightseeing, Giulia and Giuseppe are piling into their car. They are white in the face and headed on their way into the nearest town with a veterinarian. Little Trapolina, their wire-haired dachshund (whom we just adored), was swollen in the face and throat and still expanding, so it was hard for her to breathe. We fear the worst after their absence for several hours. We thought the viper had gotten to our funny-faced darling.

I couldn't relax for the rest of the evening until Giulia and Giuseppe returned. Thank God they caught the swelling in time with allergy medication for Trapolina to save her life. The following day she was unusually sluggish, rolling around in the grass, however by evening she revived and was nearly herself darting around.

We are invited for dinner our last evening. Giulia serves braised veal with customary wide egg noodles. We talked about the most customary meals of Umbria. Pork sausage of wild boars is famous here where they roam, along with Arborio rice, *risotto*. Giuseppe told of the fiasco in getting a building permit for the second-floor stairwell from the kitchen door since Italian officials took over a year even though Giuseppe is of a third generation Italian.

We feel like fast friends as Giulia pulls out a family album of photographs. She says, "My father was a pilot and died in an airplane crash." The memory still sounds guarded and raw, so I left it alone. I understand her fear of flying after losing her father and recall their help in organizing the recent air show. They wanted to admire flight from the ground. Unfortunately, it meant Giulia and Giuseppe would not be accepting our invitation to visit us in Sausalito, California.

Rapolano Terme

Neither Giuseppe nor Giulia knew of a town named Scopoli for tracing my family roots. We were in search of my grandfather's relatives of Mondi descent in this town mentioned by my father, near Perugia. My father's cousin had written a family book with the name Scopoli after visiting, however, it evaded us.

Without an answer after asking around, we decided instead to go to a local hot spring. Giulia guides us on a map that leads to a *terme*, hot spring, area which I was craving after two weeks of sightseeing and walking many kilometers. She recommends the village of Rapolano Terme with a place called Terme Antica Querciaolaia. It is a huge, age-old spa facility with at least a dozen therapy rooms and three large hot springs pools outside, of differing temperatures. I imagine how once spas had originated as a respite for Roman Soldiers after marching miles a day through battle.

My memory wanders back to childhood summer days of fun in the "World's Largest Hot Springs Pool" in Glenwood Springs, Colorado at the base of the Rocky Mountains near Aspen, before it was cosmopolitan chic. That was our childhood version of Disneyland.

The Roman Spa is an ancient traditional practice. And they certainly are the experts at serving up spas for centuries. Emperor Hadrian had one whopper of a spa in Tivoli Gardens. Today's trend of "health spas" in America, where the influence is pervasive in hotels and beauty salons and unlike the simple, original Roman spas with natural hot springs water. The phenomenon has spread like wildfire across America as a social status retreat for beauty treatments.

Calistoga in Napa County is the darling of spa towns in Northern California. I had the luxury of a thirty-minute drive from our Healdsburg home in Sonoma County through unspoiled Alexander Valley vineyards over rolling hills, past oak trees with hanging moss, arched over the road and alongside a meandering creek to Calistoga. These visits saved me and rejuvenated my body by running a ballet studio and spandex boutique. Calistoga houses over a dozen spa facilities and my favorites lie nearest the underground source of hot mineral water at Nance's, my namesake.

Unfortunately, it was badly burned in a fire and no longer retains the spa. One of the highest-rated hotel spas in the town doesn't offer the real hot springs waters but instead adds its own salts to the whirlpool bath. No thank you, I prefer Mother Nature's healing version with the magnesium and calcium salts that relax the muscles. Indian Hot Springs also provides nature's mineral springs, adjacent to former Nance's.

Checking in at our spa in Rapolano *Terme* we "rent" Italian towels which means a light cotton waffle textured cloth, not Egyptian cotton, like our version of a kitchen towel. I scheduled an appointment for a massage. The locker room is austere. All the grounds are Spartan and uncluttered. That's okay though because the pools and atmosphere more than make up for less than an absorbent towel and less than opulent surround-ings. This is a no-frills, no-nonsense, de-stressing destination that does the job. Pleasing to the eye, sensational to the bones, muscles, and mind relaxing. Sensational.

One pool has a simple fountain waterfall I stand directly under and allow the heavy stream to palpitate on my shoulders. There is very little vegetation, however, the bed of rocks with urns surrounding the pool offers a calming effect. The setting is so visually pleasing that I patterned the look beside an overflowing urn maiden fountain in my backyard in Healdsburg, California. I deemed the maiden fountain St. Madeline after my mother, watching over the terraced grapevines across from Simi Winery. She has a thumb as green as grass. I also plant urns in the ground sideways that spill out geraniums over the terrace.

By the second week of our Villa Liliana visit, I am smitten with Umbria, my heart is now tied to this landscape and region. I'm stuck like glue. We speak to Giuseppe about the possibilities of buying a home, particularly an abandoned farmhouse at the base of the hill. The could-be villa is situated on a corner, turning off the Italian cypress tree road, up toward Giuseppe's home.

Our experience of Italy from Giulia and Giuseppe's native perspective is life enriching. They both speak excellent English and were eager to share in the possibilities. We had discussed the tribulations of buying and renovating. Giuseppe introduced us to an agent. No paperwork, no deeds, no contracts. We must simply lay claim to the abandoned home that needs a ton of reconstruction and pray no grandchild (of a grandparent who lived in the home some 100 years ago), doesn't show up to claim it. The lower portion of the home was home to the animals, while upstairs was residence. You can imagine the amount of cleanup suitable for living required.

The work now seemed daunting and incomprehensible since Ray has made a living at "peddling dirt" as he calls it, most of his career with mounds of paperwork authenticating ownership as a realtor. The waiting period to lay claim is generally a year, once purchased. What if while laying the last travertine tile, planting the acre of grapevines, or installing the final piece of drywall, a proclaimed relative shows up at the door? How much do we have to pay the newfound relative to go away, or does it then turn into a timeshare at our expense?

Even Giuseppe, with third generation descendant's influence, warned, "It took us two years to get to this point on the house. There's still much for us to do with over ten rooms left to renovate. Building permits and bureaucratic oversight can be random and nonsensical." You could say that here in the United States logic is secondary by some tougher local city governments. However, in Italy, multiply that many times along with, *domani*, tomorrow procrastination.

Giuseppe suggests doing it 'The Italian Way'. Ray quizzically asks, "What is 'The Italian Way', Giuseppe?" He beams with a smirk, "That's how we've been building in Italy for centuries. We simply build, and if by slight chance are discovered, we then deal with governing impositions. So many improvements are incapable of being tracked by sheer quantity or informants, snitches like a nosey neighbor, that most go undetected."

We were also attracted by a certain invitation. Giulia spoke of a summer home in Greece where they were soon to visit and mentioned our welcome in August. The invitation had been as tantalizing as Stracciatella gelato--vanilla cream with chocolate chunks. We dashed the idea with the extravagance of returning to Europe so soon. Their warmhearted nature combined with the fact that neither of us had been to Greece kept teasing my mind like a feather softly brushing the skin.

We decide it's done, and we're off to Greece! Oooopaah! The week of our return home from Italy in the spring, the thought of passing up such a once-in-a-lifetime invitation from our wonderful Italian friends was unthinkable. A few provoking discussions ultimately led us straight to setting plans in motion for Greece in August. We thought, budget? Time? I knew where there was the will, there was a way. Realizing Giulia and Giuseppe were gracious enough to accommodate and tour us around the Ionian islands on their boat from Lefkada to Ithaca to Scorpio, Onassis private island, the decision was a no-brainer.

Late August quickly arrives, and we fly into Athens for an overnight with a rooftop view hotel across from the Acropolis, lit in amber. The following day we board Olympic Airways to the island of Lefkada. Giuseppe and Giulia greet us at the airport, and we're off to their home in the Ionian Sea, on the island of Lefkada with our own separate apartment. The location is below the heel of Italy's boot and Greece's western shores.

Where fabled Greek mythology was born, we spent the most mystical journey of my life touring islands of Greece for ten days. I was overwhelmed by our new friend's generosity and felt truly blessed to have had all the engaging, local experiences they shared with us. We were also joined by Giulia's brother who owned a house next door with friends from Switzerland and Russia. It was a remarkable international exchange for dinners at night in cafes right off the dock and the boat around the beautiful Grecian Seas.

We snorkeled nearly every morning in the blazing heat, retiring for afternoon rest for a customary three-hour nap. Off the island of Ithaca, we bravely snorkeled into underwater caves at the edge of the coast. Around the island's beaches and adjacent to jagged limestone cliffs, pure white little rocks lay perfectly rounded after tumbling through lapping waters, across the ages. Even Trapolina, Giulia's wire-haired dachshund, joined Ray in swimming, racing from shoreline to boat.

One evening we set out from Lefkada with two boats, as a group of eight to an island, near Scorpio, where Onassis entertained Opera Diva Maria Callas and later in life perhaps, Jacqueline Kennedy-Onassis and family. A couple of the guys went spearfishing. For dinner, we docked and jumped out to a restaurant standing right on the water for a classic Greek meal drenched in olive oil.

As dark descended and the midnight blue sky washed over us, we stopped in the middle of the sea with the stars and sky like a giant globe above. We dove into the deep dark waters below, skinny dipping, and looked above to the stars that twinkled like no other place on earth. The quiet and calm transported me into a sense of serendipity. The magic of Greece permeates time and soon our Grecian adventure came to a perfect finale. We flew out on September 9, 2001, a day earlier than scheduled through New York and then home.

After a day of recuperating jet lag, the unthinkable occurred on September 11, 2001. Waking up with espresso, we sat stunned on the sofa in front of the TV to the tragedy unfolding all morning. As the two jets bombed into the towers, Ray remained frozen on the sofa in front of the screen nearly all day. We understood then that life, as we knew it in America, had forever changed. I prayed that day, thanking God for such a blessing in timing to return home the day before this without a glitch. Buying a home in Italy now seemed altogether too distant and risky, since no one knew what economic and international repercussions would unfold with the results of the devastation.

My mind wanders back to my departing day from Umbria where I took special notice of the birds in the long row of Italian cypress trees. One such bird I named the "Go-Away" bird, took the lead in front of the car, weaving in and out of the saluting cypress trees that lined the entire length of the long dirt road leading towards beautiful Lake Trasimeno. Dodging and darting in front of our car within the height of the trees as if an advance scout.

I was mesmerized by the determination to lead and escort us on our way out. This marvelous bird was another Divine sign for our return visit.

It was as if Go-Away bird was saying:

Glad you enjoyed your stay,

Let me escort your way,

A departing magical display.

On this memorable last day,

Please come again and play.

Chapter 4

Veni, Vidi, Vici, All Roads Lead to Roma

I came, I saw, I conquered…The Italian spirit is like a bird in flight soaring with faith and imagination on the wings of Da Vinci. Where does the Italian spirit soar? Italy provides the presence of a spiritual quality and the passion of feeling fully alive. Italians say you must experience Italy, not explain it.

A favorite Da Vinci quote: "*The noblest pleasure is the joy of understanding.*"

Both the ecstasy and agony of Roma is well characterized in Respighi's symphony *Pines of Rome and Fountains of Rome.*

We flew from home in San Francisco, California to Roma in the Spring of 2001. Venturing out on our first day along Via Dei Fori Imperiali, Ray and I found a crew busily setting up street bleachers for an event of monumental proportion adjacent to the Forum Arena of Ruins. Italian Liberation Day is *domani*, tomorrow, and greets our arrival. A military parade will be marching through the main artery of Roma. As an American, I feel deeply appreciated, when engaging them with my understanding of very few Italian words. Their smiles, gestures and embrace, which Italians regularly bestow is a warm welcome.

During this period of world tension, just seven months after September 11, the Italians share with me a loyalty to American soldiers for sparing their country and Europe during World War II. Italian Liberation Day is celebrated as a National Holiday on April 25 during our visit. I can read it in their expressive eyes, their gaze of gratefulness--fortuitous to be here at this moment in time. Nowhere in Europe during all my travels, were more words of gratitude shown to us for this time and place in history. Beaming with pride, the gesturing Italians act as welcoming diplomats.

Near the Roman Forum, at Piazza Venezia, a sturdy horse and carriage came clopping up with driver Brutus whose name is perfectly appropriate sitting in the circle drive awaiting his next visitor for touring. Bruno is a brute, bearing the body of a finely chiseled athlete, a modern-day gladiator. Bruno wants to charge an arm and a leg to take the tour. Italians just say arm, *braccio.* I haggled the price with this man-machine and got a reasonable rate to run the course of the ruins in our Chariot driven by Ben Hur ala 21st Century. Bruno, Bruno, Bruno -- his giant bald head atop muscles bulging from his neck and arms- steers his horse, *il cavallo* through traffic with the ease of a chariot champion. Gladiator blood is coursing through his veins.

Touring around Roma with modern chariot driver Bruno by Roman landmarks with umbrella pines above.

Turns out his finesse to rein the draft horse and command his steed through the collision course of crazy Roman drivers and blocked parade lanes around the Roman Forum to the Coliseum is effortlessly choreographed. We weave in and out of buses and autos as if this were the chariot he drove for competition inside the Coliseum in ages past. Where modern mixes with ancient, he shouts out the sights, barely audible from the horse's clopping. Bruno was our Ben Hur. His build is like the sturdy draft horse, snapping his whip in hand and clippity, clop, clop, clop, off we go.

We canter around our days' conquest of sightseeing. The umbrella pines strike a pose, lining Piazza Venezia along Vittorio Emmanuelle. The gaze of envious tourists at the luxury of our own private chariot brings a grin within and gratefulness for saving miles of walking.

It reminds me of a day strolling in Manhattan Theatre District to see a Broadway play when a horse-drawn carriage driven by a darling coachman approached me and asked, "Where can I take you today, dear lady?" I responded, "To see *Evita.*" He pulled up in front of all the patrons and produced the royal escort extended hand and bow entrance for me. Without a ticket, I instinctively chasse' past hundreds of patrons waiting in line to the front with some nerve and got my ticket at the counter instantly. After that entrance, how could I possibly go to the back of the line? This was a role tonight I thoroughly relished and waltzed right into the theater lobby.

Back along Via Dei Fori Imperiali metal bleachers are stacked and lined up in anticipation of the parade. Italian Liberation Day is a military parade. The marching happens tomorrow in appreciation of Italian and American Troops of war. Past the Roman Forum, Circus Maximus, and round The Roman Coliseum, my imagination is roused by the dark caverns that appear as holding cells for the gladiators and beasts, and horrid thoughts of such a hedonistic society. The beauty of Brutus' chariot covering ground past so many monuments, saving these weary legs and swollen feet, is a grand reward and brings a sigh of relief as I jump from his chariot.

The city I observe speaks of an advanced civilization and the lands speak of conquest. The aqueducts brought survival during war and the building of palaces brought royal eccentricity. During the rule of emperors such as Tiberius, Nero and Caligula, coliseums entertained in gruesome glory for the sport of killing man and beast. It was a diversion for the people to distract them from the emperor's gluttony, greed and excess which eventually led to the downfall of Roman Civilization. Today's Rome cultivates an ever inspiring and intimate relationship with its past. Greek civilization was highly influential to the Romans and the synthesis developed Italian society. Today they cherish the devotion within their own twenty regions and nation.

Ingenuity exploded, flowing into the world's art and architecture. Roman history reminds today's modern society that Christian behavior is a key component to an enduring, civilized society. Pope Pius XI assured such during the war, by drawing numerous pacts with Mussolini for the Vatican's separation of state. The Pope also insured Catholic education in public schools. The discipline and focus of "Do unto others as you would have them do unto you" became engrained in the Italian mind and maintains civility in Italian Society.

Creation of a Glorious Culture

Each time I return to Italy, I find the sphere of Italian influence is so vast yet we in America are only vaguely aware of how much Italians evolved to fashion our everyday lives. Italian culture continues to share with the world its everlasting genius in art, architecture, faith, performing arts, literature, design, fashion, science, medicine, engineering, farming, cuisine, religion, and family devotion. I have merely scratched the surface of the marble block that has shaped and sculpted Italian life.

During the period of enormous revival known as The Renaissance, Popes, royalty, and the affluent commissioned artists to create some of the world's greatest works of art and architecture, by families such as the renowned Medici. This remarkable period from the 1400s to the 1600s was when Italy brought magnificence to its people. Because so much regard was given to artistic endeavors and family, rather than full focus on war and conquest, a new civilization was born out of the Renaissance.

The creative genius of artist Michelangelo flourished in Renaissance times. A lesser-known story is that he idolized a less familiar sculptor today, the Greek sculptor who most inspired his creations. Michelangelo modeled the movement and muscular definition he made famous, after the Laocoon sculpture. The sculpture Laocoon was named after the Trojan priest who warned his people not to accept the Trojan horse, a masterpiece that showed incredible motion and evoked unsurpassed emotion. Laocoon was found in Roma by accident while unearthing sites in the early 1500s.

In 1506 Laocoon inspired the beginning of the Vatican Museums when acquired by Pope Julius II.

As unbelievable as it may seem, when Michelangelo was asked to sculpt and restore the *braccia*, missing arms, on the sculpture Laocoon, he refused. He said his ability was not up to the mastery of Greek creation. The masterpiece brought a newfound zeal to the artists of The Renaissance, who then looked back at Roma for its ancient glory.

The Vatican

Italy proudly boasts half of the world's fine art. Vatican City alone, which is the world's smallest country/state, houses more frescoes, paintings, sculptures, and scripts within its museums than one can study in a lifetime. One of many return visits remains a testament to the glory of Rome, especially when staying just a few blocks away from the Vatican.

What stood out most surprisingly is the number of shops selling religious artifacts for priests and churches. Chalices, altarpieces, vestments, statues, and too many to mention, ornamented the windows. Rosaries are strung out on carousel display racks with beads of every color and stone. I purchase a few for family members. I wonder how many Our Father and Hail Mary prayers have been said here on The Vatican grounds through the years. An infinite number?

A Divine happenstance occurred with a Mass just starting by a Cardinal in one of the side altars of St. Peters Basilica. We were prompted to participate while surrounded by saintly spirits and solemn prayer, the awesome spirituality within the walls of St. Peters offers a significant tribute to history through religious ages. I will dearly hold this Mass celebration eternally close to my heart.

My hope and expectation of seeing the Swiss Guards are rewarded. They must be Swiss born. The uniform is a costume in today's attire. They are Medici colors, so vivid, particularly the royal blue stripe. I blink at the stunning outfit and posture as straight as their sword. The sword-like halberd, spike on a pole, and surety of the soldier's stance bring to mind the ancient weapons of jousting warfare. The armor is from the 15th century.

I want to return as a pilgrimage, our last Sunday when Pope John Paul II, aka JP II, appears for up to 50,000 pilgrims in Vatican Square. JP II greets his faithful most every Sunday from the Papal Window. After our first couple of days in Rome and traveling across Italy for two weeks, we return to Rome for a Vatican pilgrimage before our departure.

That Sunday in Piazza San Pietro, I feel the religious fervor and charge in the air. Groups waving banners for Pope Saint John Paul II, written in their native language, designate their church, city, and country back home. Chants erupt for the Pope, particularly by the Italians singing "Il Papa Giovanni, Il Papa Giovanni." Everyone is posed to face the tiny window where he'll appear from his Papal Suite second floor up.

We are standing a football stadium distance from the Papal residence and a silent hush over thousands this sunny Spring Day. A giant red banner unfurls from the frame of the window like a magic carpet. A capped head pops in front of the window and from our distance, his head is the size of a penny. Not exactly box seats, however, the presence of His Eminence is enough to light up another meaningful moment in my life with the grandness of the Roman Catholic Church's Vicar of Christ with 1.3 billion believers. I felt a bit closer to redemption since being a wayward Catholic in years past.

Pope Saint John Paul II, endearingly known as JP II is the most beloved and venerated Pope, certainly of our time, perhaps all time. His most important mission was to travel and reach out to the whole world with his message of peace and love, particularly the youth as he treads in his Converse tennies.

Not surprisingly, Pope Saint John Paul II admired St. Augustine who wrote, *"The world is a book, and those who do not travel, read only one page."* St. Augustine believed in the inherent goodness of man to earn salvation with the Church as the spiritual city of God distinct from the material city of man. I deem Pope Saint John Paul II as The King of Hearts in The World of Italy.

Roma *Ristorante* Restaurant

One evening Ray and I sauntered through the streets of Rome in quest of just the right restaurant for atmosphere with plenty of local diners, real Roman residents, a sign of *buona* local fare. The aromas from *ristorante* to *osteria* were so enticing, my tongue was salivating. We were conditioned to eating dinner at least two hours earlier and feeling starved. Combined with the added eight-hour time zone, you can imagine the appetite we had after a day's whirlwind of sightseeing. Italian dinnertime starts around eight in the evening or *otto di sera*.

Entering a warm and busy *trattoria* with white linen-draped tables in a casually chic atmosphere, the aroma and banter of patrons won us over. When asked to be seated, we were escorted to a table that was both teeny-tiny and in the way of kitchen traffic and clanging dishes, so we requested a move to another table.

The waiter demonstrated with great emotion the table we pointed to was reserved and unavailable. Yet not five minutes later, a much younger and casual American couple who clearly just strolled in, were seated at the very table we requested. Without reservation, the waiter's mood, so adamant the table was reserved, just like the wind, had shifted.

Such Commedia dell'Arte is in my vocabulary, "Italianism." Whatever change of mind, fits the mood, gets their goat, turns them on, or sets you free. This is the way decisions are often made in Italy, sometimes even of the highest order and consequence. They are truly masters of improvisation.

The waiter just didn't feel like seating us there at that particular moment. Italians feel no need to apologize, and with all their inbred hospitality you easily overlook it. Throw rhyme or reason out the door. You better start off giggling and resign yourself to some idiosyncrasies of *Italianos*.

The next night we found another delectable meal and sat by Peter, Pietro, the shoe salesman for Formula-One race car drivers. I had no idea, such a living existed. He came from Pescara, Abruzzo in the same region as my grandmother, Antonia. Pietro's formula driver shoes are created similarly to ballet slippers and made to fit like gloves. His family's trade signifies the lost art and pride in handing down from one generation to the next such a specialty trade in a shoe. The goals and joy in their business are not as much about income as they are about the refined detail in the handcrafted beauty of their work with family dedication through many years. Shedding light on time is not necessarily money. These are the artisans.

The sleek Ferrari's speed and the need to push the pedal to the metal in Italians is considered fine art and a trait of their driving. The contradiction lies in the Italian slow casual, relaxed lifestyle, and methods of most businesses. Italians have dubbed much of their cuisine "slow food" in disapproval of America's fast-food frenzy without fresh, healthy cooking.

The cuisine is undoubtedly one of Italy's finest ongoing contributions to world culture. I cannot help but touch a bit on it. However, there is so much more studied and written by chefs that I'm inclined to give just a few sprinkles about food to spice it up. The aroma of ragu, grilling pancetta with parmesan and olive oil, and the sweet scent of basil and fennel seasonings permeate my sense of smell while strolling the streets during *passeggiate,* an evening stroll that is ritual-like religion to the community.

One simply cannot eat poorly at any street café or *trattoria*, even if you dislike pasta and tomato sauce. *Trattorias* and *osterias* are where you'll find the local Italians if you don't want to be surrounded by other hotel guests. The fashionable restaurants are a feast to the eyes and palate, particularly when they spread antipasto situated like a salad bar. There is a delectable selection with everything from roasted tomato to calamari and mouthwatering vegetables grilled in herbs of fennel, basil, rosemary, parsley, and oregano.

Café Bars are social gatherings where serving espresso, macchiato, cappuccino, gelato, confections, and brandies, has existed for centuries. Less traveled Americans and younger generations seem to think coffee bars are a newfound social phenomenon, when they have been an Italian tradition for centuries. Café Greco in Roma has been serving up coffee since 1760 and is posh.

Italians live larger than life with their love for Grand Opera onstage and off as well in their daily lives. They stir up passion and awaken the senses. Italians love a certain element of chaos. They have a saying for beautiful confusion--*Un bello confusione.* To be Italian is to be ambivalent, particularly true with foreigners. Like a woman, Italians want the prerogative to change their minds in any given circumstance. I call it Italianism. Italians have their own hand language in gestures, not unlike sign language. Author Bernini personifies this in *The Italians.*

Italian Commedia dell'Arte is whimsical entertainment. Their language was determined by the beauty of its cadence, the Florentine style of Dante's *Divine Comedy,* and established by the intellectuals of the 16th Century. The uplifting lilt of the language sounds like singing poetry.

Veni, Vidi, Vici. I came, I saw, I conquered my fears of the big cities and the unknown of country life. Discovering how Italian innovation and culture contribute to our lives, the spirit of the artisans, and the vibrancy of everyday Italians, absorbing the joy in their lives has filled my spirit.

It reminds me back home how consumed with accumulating and confused we Americans have become, losing the nature of our purpose and the nurture of our hearts. The Italian spirit is in my heart calling me to return *ancora e ancora*, again, and again….

Chapter 5

A Divine Moment and The Twilight Zone in Roma

A ray of powdery sunlight beams down like a spotlight from heaven, through the apex of the gigantic *duomo*, dome. The sun is shining brilliantly where light and air filter through the oculus. Everything inside including the visitors beneath and around the rotunda lingers on the edges of dark shadows in a mystical aura. The Pantheon is the most extraordinary model of ancient glory in Roma.

The Pantheon wears two thousand years of age like Papal Power. Originally built as a pagan temple to the gods, Christians deemed it their own to save from pagan destruction and proceeded through the centuries to bury many Popes within the walls. This building breathes a sense of the ancient weighing down through its massive, thick walls and dome of history since 1 AD.

In total contrast to the heaviness of history under the dark shadows, and stained dome shines a heavenly light through the aperture where a circular apex is atop the dome. This divine structure opens portals of the past. As I stand beneath this oculus, out of the worldly realm, a single pure, white feather materializes in sight, balanced in the aperture, and begins its descent from the opening of the dome. Starting at the point of the aperture, pirouetting, and floating downward in a spiral slow motion. As the symbol of peace, this feather from a white dove embodies spiritual peacefulness and permeates the air throughout the *Duomo.* Such a Divine moment reminds me of the Luminous Mysteries of the rosary...*Behold the heavens were opened and He saw the spirit of God descending like a dove.* Matthew 3:16

The light little feather above us, never veers outside of the powdery light ray, spiraling, and dancing in its descent. Spiral after spiral, the feather, like an aerial gymnast winds its way down. As if choreographed to the music of *The Dying Swan*, the flight seems the length of the cello's chant. The graceful ballet of the feather pays tribute to the Italian and Papal Monarchy resting in the walls of The Pantheon as a dance through time.

Throughout the feathers descending dance, I could hear the Adagio of the Cello resonate the solitary sighs, reverberating like a murmur beating through the heart. How that feather magically danced through the spotlight and the music in my mind. Time stood still in this graceful Divine Moment. As the feather lands and lays in the circle of light on the ground, this feather from above is something too spiritual and supernatural to take. So, I left it to rest.

Serendipity.

Another magnificent vision is a tradition Christians celebrate at Pentecost with the descent of the Holy Spirit upon the Apostles, the seventh Sunday after Easter. On this special Holy Day in Roma at The Pantheon, a spectacle for the senses is celebrated by a shower of rose petals representing the red flames, a symbol of the Holy Spirit above the Apostle's heads. The rose petals float down from the top of the dome oculus and through the light into The Pantheon, filling the faithful with a vision in breathless awe.

The Twilight Zone in Rome

I'm ready for the ultimate Italian Dramatic Performance in Rome. The Opera Diva in *Tosca* and the tenacious Tenor. I dress in my evening best and wear a red poppy dress with a flirty skirt that dances as I step. From visiting Covent Garden, London to Rio de Janeiro, Brazil's Opera House, a replica of the Paris Opera House, my days of pirouetting as a ballet dancer and instructor now move me to visit Opera Houses and Theatres where inspired music, opera, and ballet history still thrive in most of these centuries old Opera Houses. Unlike most historical buildings, today Opera Houses serve the same purpose as originally built where I can feel the musical and theatrical spirit still alive and breathing through the walls.

After pounding the pavement of at least seven shoe stores along Via Cola di Rienzo shopping boulevard I finally find a pair of black sleek heeled sandals and my outfit is now complete. Italians have gifted us shoes as Masters of leather shoemaking going back to Roman gladiator sandals, even finding the right sandal for comfort and size is a challenge. Euro sizing does not easily convert into American sizes, who have bigger, wider feet overall.

Fashion ready and right in step to take the limo from our hotel to the Opera House, I await with the excitement of fulfilling a yearning of many years. *Tosca* is the Opera advertised with beautiful little billets showing the moon rising over a *Duomo*, a cathedral dome. The billets are posted on the Pillars in our Rome hotel lobby.

Giacomo Puccini is one of Italy's most prolific composers. Tosca is celebrating one hundred years of existence. And so en route to the Opera, the games begin. The limo turns out to be a shuttle bus and arrives half an hour late. The price of $65 a ticket, or however many lire at the time, including transportation should have been a tip-off. We are shuttled to at least six other hotel stops throughout Rome before arriving at the Opera.

We have been riding in the bus for nearly 90 minutes and still not at the Opera. It seems we keep driving further and further to the outskirts of town into the residential ghetto of Rome. Some of the thirty or so of us stunned passengers on the bus are getting a queasy feeling for a ride out of the Twilight Zone at this twilight hour as the sun sets.

Everyone is dressed very smartly as an international representation of Opera aficionados. Heads keep turning and looks of concern and confusion are increasing from the passengers on our bus. There are attendees from Australia, France, and Germany, who look sharp and sophisticated. We finally arrive at a nondescript cement building from about the 1950s surrounded by a neighborhood of impoverished buildings. This is no Opera House. As we shuffle out of the bus with mumblings and giant question marks on our faces, the first exclamation of "Uh-Oh" is voiced. The tenement buildings are too close for comfort and an eerie quiet of 'what are we in for now' feeling descends upon us as we hesitatingly step into an elementary school auditorium, about as appealing as cafeteria lunch.

We're all looking at each other filing in as the auditorium starts to fill with 200 in attendance. They surprisingly escort us in two by two after our ticket dates were closely scrutinized. The theater of theatrics is being played upon us as if we were VIP. Perhaps that is to avoid a rumble. In speaking to the Australians next to us, we begin to burst out laughing because we're captive with nowhere to go. All 200 plus of us have been duped. After all, I mark it up as another Italianism, for in their minds if no one is hurt and the charade is a success, Bravo!

Before the curtains even open, we look around and wonder how to get a cab back into the city of Rome. This is the kind of neighborhood you don't want to step out at night and look to even hail a cab. The amazing thing is how accommodating everyone on staff appeared. An arrangement was announced, "If you'd like to take a cab back to your hotel, there is a sign-up list, and the cabs should arrive at intermission." Obviously for those already on to the heist. Tosca hasn't even started and a line for the sign-up is nearly one-third of the auditorium. What a science these masters of dupedom have crafted. We've all resigned to tolerating the next two and one-half hours of opera. I mention to Ray, “How bad can it be since we’re at least in Italy with Italian Opera Singers?” Maybe the talent will make up for the space.

Well, I smell something further afoul. The curtains open. It’s bad to worse. The lead female, Floria Tosca is Asian. No there is no Bravissimo except to the degree of being taken for a detour on a long night. My dream of seeing an Italian Opera with beautiful, authentic Italian voices and faces is a fiasco extraordinaire.

By the second act, it’s so bad I suggest we leave and go sit in the bus and wait, along with many others who are exiting to their awaiting buses. As suspected, not a single cab came to the rescue. We prefer the silence or company of strangers over sitting through the rest of this disaster called Opera. Our happiness in the bus at that point is the relief of knowing we are within an hour’s time of heading back to Rome.

The next day I am determined to confront the hotel manager and give him a piece of my mind. “We were held hostage for five hours of precious, costly travel time in Italy,” I exclaimed. I thought some compensation, at least an explanation is in order for sending us on a fiasco that has been expensive not only in cost but in time -every moment is precious. The hotel did the booking, and I booked the hotel through an airline agent in the U.S. How could they represent such deception?

No one, of course, took responsibility and the manager listened with pleasant intent as if he understood that this should never occur. He merely double talked his way around. What was to be our first Opera attended in Italy and “Do as The Romans Do” turned into a Commedia dell’Arte of the first order. What can you do but laugh at the comedy and tragedy of it all?

Mind you, this degree of trickery is rare in my experience of Italy, and only once have I been blundered into such an extensive heist out of countless bookings for hotels, rentals, tours, and transportation. A learning experience of the highest order. Italianism is the art of showmanship.

If a van or bus appears at your hotel requiring many stops with other captive passengers for the opera, quickly turn on your toes and high tail it to the nearest *bene ristorante,* a nice restaurant. You might ask your waiter to sing *Nessun Dorma,* he probably will at close to the level of singing in an opera. Lesson? Check and recheck your sources in Italy. Bravissimo Roma.

Raymond with pizza in viaggio, on the go

Chapter 6

Firenze, Florence, Fantastico

Since my first trip to Italy is flying solo, *Firenze* becomes my lure. Florence is much more manageable than say, Rome or Venice by size and crowds. The city of *Firenze* boasts housing one-third of Italy's fine art. Even more incredible still, over half of the world's fine art is in Italy alone. The Medici Family's 300 year reign in Florence during The Renaissance produced more art than any other era in man's history. Painting, sculpture, murals, mosaics, and architecture were fiercely competitive due to commissions from royalty and guilds.

The city captured my heart when I saw the film, *A Room with a View* in the late 1980s. Romantic in a love story and romantic in artistic beauty and nature. Being single and distraught by a recent boyfriend breakup whom I thought was the one, I was undeterred and driven to overcome my fears. All the better to escape into the romantic nature of travel. I prayed not to become forlorn or soppy.

Firenze, Florence is the heart of Italian artistic nature, a place of beauty where art and architectural triumphs are commonplace. Florence is at the heart of Italy where the greatest gift to the world is Renaissance art.

I began this venture with my feisty leprechaun sized Irish friend Shawn. She and I wanted to first see the chic of Paris and soak up the golden coast, Cote D'Azur, along the French Riviera. They were splendid days of fine arts and Riviera nightlife.

One early morning in our hotel while swimming laps on the rooftop pool overlooking the Mediterranean, I struck up a conversation with another early bird. He happened to be there producing Madonna's concert in Nice at an enormous stadium. He was kind enough to offer backstage tickets, so I thought why not? I came back to the room to awaken Shawn and jumping like a maniac, I exclaim, "Can you believe we live in Los Angeles and here we score tickets for a Madonna concert in Nice, France?" As a dancer, of course, was most interested in her trend-setting stage choreography.

The next morning, I stopped at the hotel reception, and sure enough, the deskman produced two lanyard IDs for backstage. That evening we hail a cab to be deposited outside a soccer stadium ticket area and are directed to proceed behind the stage area. We waltz through the ground seats and come to a blockade where like the waters of the Red Sea, the partition parts. Wo-o-oa-ah! I snap a look at Shawn, "We get free rein to roam backstage." Well, we were underwhelmed by the vulgar and violent display causing Madonna's tour to be banned in Italy. We got a kick out of standing next to actor Bruce Willis, however.

Shawn and I separated in Nice as I was off to Italy solo, while she journeyed back home to visit her mother in Bantry, Ireland, the southernmost fishing port of Cork County.

Following our French venture, I departed from the train in Nice along the beautiful coastal Mediterranean. I sat dazed on the ride, gazing into a crystal sea from the window's view. I'm astonished at the clarity of the water since centuries of humanity have resided on the shores.

Somehow, I missed my connection to Florence and ended up in Roma. It was late evening, so I offered it up to destiny and decided to see as much of Rome in one evening as possible. My tour turned out to be *magnifico*, magnificent, by way of taking a night bus tour. It was stunning and mysterious to see the lighting and completely different mood of Roma's landmarks by night. The stage lighting of The Trevi Fountain and Colosseum is dramatic and breathtaking.

The next day, through the chaos of the Roma train terminal, and delayed arrival to Florence, I wearily checked into a hotel just across from the Palazzo Vecchio. The evening seemed to celebrate my arrival with a window view over rooftops, and candles lighting up the *campanile, bell* tower balcony of the Palazzo Vecchio like a birthday cake. The tower stood only thirty yards away. In between every opening of brickwork on the tower turret landings, flames flickered.

I called down to reception asking about the significance of the candles atop the tower. "*Giorno Italiano Liberazione*" he announces, Italian Liberation Day, "when America freed Italy from Fascism." I already feel special about this surprise birthday cake in tribute to my home country and Italy's freedom. I later learned the palace has been at the heart of political life. The campanile bell rang out for Parlamento, Parliament, and public gatherings.

The next morning, I entered The Academia Museum, the world's first art studio and Florence's finest showcase of art. How could the colossal statue of David rise from one enormous block of marble were it not for the yearning to live life larger? A favorite quote of Michelangelo: "I saw the angel in the marble and carved until I set him free."

Sculpture speaks to me more than any other visual art form. The movement and three-dimensional quality beckon me to reach out and touch. The derriere of David looks exquisite. With all the marble monuments in Florence, sculptures alone would keep me busy for weeks in this Renaissance Capital.

As I stared in amazement, I came to one particularly poignant female sculpture with her own salon. At this point nature was calling quickly and I needed to find the quickest toilet exit. Just behind me in the salon was an exit door marked ever so discreetly. Not having seen the "Emergency Exit Only" sign, pushing against the door, I set off the alarm in The Academia.

The blaring sound prompted the visitors to cover their ears. Immediately from the next room came the guard in uniform, wielding his baton and wearing a grin. I tried to gesture with my hands to express my need for the *bagno,* bathroom and he directed me by the elbow to the proper closest exit.

Onto personal matters, buying black leather pants for the fashionable Los Angeles Twentieth Century Fox Film Premiere Parties is my shopping quest. The salesman, Guido thought my then size 4 petite body could fit into a size 2. As liberally as I dressed back then, even these painted-on size 2 leather pants gave me a "lamppost" look. Opting for size 4, Guido offered me a discount in lira, back in the day before Euros, 1989. This exchange equated to a mere $100, and I suspect that Guido was fishing for a date with such a discount.

I wasn't particularly enthralled and a bit leery. However, I thought this would be a good way to see how an Italian worker goes about his day. We set a safer lunch date and before we even arrived at lunch, he proceeded to hold his jaw in hand and complain of his toothache and lack of money for dental work. Not exactly my picture of *A Roman Holiday*, already requesting financial help.

I quickly dismissed Guido's theatrical performance with his hand to jaw in pain, inhaled lunch, and bid him Ciao. That dashed my ideas of any future romantic rendezvous with the very 'hands-on' Italian men. Armed with my Los Angeles dating days armor, even if his misfortune was genuine, his immediate disclosure made me most uncomfortable. Such an approach was hardly my idea of travel romance, as I was looking for beauty on my first venture to Italy.

As I departed Florence on board the train, I noticed a particularly angelic young boy leading his younger sister to her seat. The brother, about twelve years of age, handily escorted his sister, about seven years old, to her seat. He spent almost ten minutes putting her baggage in the overhead, gently handing her the ticket, and sitting next to her, tenderly touching her face as if he were saying goodbye to a love for a long while. As he departed the train, he stood outside her window and held his gaze until he was a mere speck back at the station.

Such an act of brotherly love I have never witnessed before from a young boy and knew in the hearts of the Italians this was a scene that may not be uncommon. An act of love seared in my brain. Most American children would think it strange to show such affection for a sibling and would not waste their precious self-time. Not cool for a brother.

On my next trip to Florence one year later, I find a true view of The Arno in a *pensione,* an Italian Inn. Watching the scull boats in the river this morning gives me an instant reminder of awakening in a foreign country. I envision the river as a highway for the ships and boats back as far as 50 A.D. with Roman soldiers returning from their conquests and boatloads filled with spoils. My grand size room and bed with flimsy mattress and springs carry me in a drift to medieval times.

Many years later in 2001, during a day trip to *Firenze,* Florence via train from Passignano on the shore of Lake Trasimeno, I recall this solo venture. On this later trip to Florence, after a raucous night of vino and celebrating with our guests in the spectacular view villa above the lake, we made our way by car down hairpin turns to the train station, arriving in Florence at 10:30 AM. The Firenze is overcast, soon awash in rain. The weather resembled my overcast feeling. Shopping and sightseeing *chiesa*, churches, The Duomo, etc. made for one quick day by train from our villa in Umbria. Running between store canopy harbors, we view The Medici monarch's influence upon this city appearing around every corner.

Sandro Botticelli, Michelangelo Buonarroti, and Leonardo DaVinci were fiercely competitive contemporaries, as was the entire art community from late 1400 to early 1500s. The Medici's were determined to breathe life into a new civilization through artistic beauty for mankind throughout everlasting history. Mission accomplished beyond all imagination and eras.

While along the promenade of The Uffizi Gallery, two magnificently costumed *pulcinella*, clowns or mimes, took pictures of people on a tufted, ornate stool holding a gilded picture frame around the subject's face while the mime companion shot the photo. Their antics were cleverly choreographed. One wore red and white polka dots and a dunce clown cap with white gloves and large brown shoes. On his white face, his red, carrot-like nose protruded. The other clown looked like the classic mime in all white with red pom poms down the front of his costume and a white skull cap.

I was so giddy when Ray sat on the throne to be photographed, that when handing over our digital camera, it slipped from my grasp and took a slow-motion tumble down the steps, never to shoot a picture again.

Moving on to shopping, I find a delicate porcelain swan of a thousand feathers from a contemporary famous Italian sculptor, a graceful reminder of Ballet's Swan Lake. I have a fondness for the gracefulness of swans. The gorgeous full bloom rose size piece floats in lightness for the creature it portrays. Giuseppe Armani of Florence is a gifted sculptor. The piece was irresistible, a masterpiece.

My heart was set on a leather jacket as the major purchase this vacation. We ran and leapt across wet running water alleyways from shop to shop, ducking into a leather boutique out of the rain. With the shop and owner all to ourselves, I began my search through the layered racks of leather jackets. So many colors and styles in one small boutique the likes I'd never seen, made it difficult in the choosing.

The kind middle-aged gentleman with a brown beard and shoulder-length hair remarks, "My jackets are purchased by a few of the larger upscale department stores like Saks, back in the United States." I decided on a burgundy color which became my favored jacket that season. The new skin fit fabulously. Velvety soft and supple to the touch, with a pleasant aroma of earthiness as Italian artisans are ever so famous for producing.

The skies burst with rain that late afternoon and kept us from outdoor sights. Running through puddles and under awnings from shop to shop, and a prayer stop in one *chiesa,* church, makes for a melancholy memory. We scurry to the train station by six in the evening and collapse onto the train's backseat on our way to the Villa.

Chapter 7

Escape from the Albanians

I have seldom experienced days in my travels that have been more unnerving and astonishing, than this journey. My flight into Milan from San Francisco gives me a few days to decompress after a flight crossing both the United States and the Atlantic Ocean. Before heading to the French Riviera, I hope to shed my jet lag in Milan while squeezing in a bit of window shopping and sightseeing. Milan provides a visual smorgasbord to looking fabulous, *Bella Figura*, the art of beautiful people watching in the world of high fashion. Appearance is everything and as important as the food you eat, according to the Milanese.

The Milan train station is Gigantor. I picture two prehistoric mammoths like marble pillars supporting the ceiling beams with their enormous tusks. The cavernous terminal stands two stories high with escalators, vaulted ceilings, and marble columns. Our wait of fifteen minutes in line for first-class tickets produced general seating, we later find out, being unaware that reserved seats require a specific request to have your name posted, or so we were later told.

The journey to the French Riviera is a full day with many stops making for a long, long, full day. This is the weekend of the sensational Grand Prix de Monte Carlo.

Therefore, at nearly every stop, we are jostled about playing musical chairs from seat to seat. Without our name posted above the seats, we are at the mercy of the next passenger to board with their named reservation. I am exhaustibly irritated since the ticket agent did not properly advise our first-class options. The porter swaggers down the center aisle and appears to have been riding the *vino*, wine express for some time. When I stand up and demand an answer for continually being displaced, he merely huffs in my face to say, "No *capisco.*" I don't understand English. The sensory overload of his bad breath came fuming out and knocks me into my seat once again.

After all the bumping around we feel like tomatoes on a produce truck. An observant couple from Australia, seeing my distress, share concerns in the Italian spirit of things. Genoa is where we collide with Max and Diana, the Australians, amidst all the fatiguing seat hopping. Max takes command and tells the next passengers boarding that the seats now vacant across from them, are ours. He is well-versed in train travel and Europe in general. Max is a manufacturer of fine athletic wear in Europe. The way they sported their own well-groomed attire speaks of a designer sportswear.

Max and I switch seats so that he can talk man to man with Ray. I exchange a few words with Diana, who is very quiet. Soon Max shouts across the aisle to Diana, "Did you tell her?" Diana shakes her head no and Max proceeds to let us in on their harrowing ordeal of the past 48 hours. No wonder Diana was quiet. They surely don't wear their exhaustion since being alert to helping us with extraordinary kindness. Their show of compassion, as that of Italians, is contagious.

Max explains that in Florence, while checking into their grand luxury hotel and backing up the rental car, he slightly bumps the car behind him. An Albanian passenger pops out from between the cars, complaining of hitting his leg. No further ado was made as they all walked away from the incident unscathed.

Max explains, "The following day, the hotel manager advises them that the Albanian has brothers who have already complained to the hotel desk. The Albanians were threatening and harassing with so-called injuries, hospitalization, and looking for compensation from the auto bump to his leg the day before. Like henchmen."

My mind flashes back to an incident I experienced in Los Angeles while driving. I bumped a car in the rear end at a busy stop and go traffic stop and without a dent, everyone walked away. Many harassing phone calls and a lawsuit later from an undocumented driver, who claimed neck injuries, reminded me of the burden. The similarity ends there.

The look on their faces as they reveal the nightmarish experience describing the level of threat to them is frightening. Even after their horrible escapade, Max was right there to help us in our seating upheaval scenario. The good-natured Italians tend to bring out the warmth in everyone.

As Max and Diana's story unfolded, the hotel manager, in order to divert any danger to them, took it upon himself to warn Max and Diana to steal away in the middle of the night. Max and Diana escaped first to Bologna on a night train, where they checked into a hotel with an alias. The following day they again boarded a train enroute to Nice to leave Italy for more assured safety.

Bravo to Italian attentiveness and hospitality. With their hearts in the right place when bad things happen, the hotel management dealt with protecting their guests. In all my days traveling within Italy, I felt safe that someone would come to the rescue, at least offer assistance in a crisis.

Max said, "I wish we were American now, there is no Australian Embassy. It is times like these when we really need an embassy." Knowing nothing of Embassy protocol I assumed there wasn't a thing we could do to intervene but bring some sanity and company back to their world. It was critical for them to get out of Italy and lose the Albanians as they were out for big money or blood. Perhaps both.

Despite their whirlwind traverse across Italy and being awake over forty-eight hours on the run with their last few drops of adrenalin, we engaged in upbeat, lively conversation. Max and Ray set an overnight plan since neither of us had hotel reservations. We smacked ideas about like a hearty match of volleyball. Max got busy on his cell phone with his business manager in Australia. His task is to find a hotel room in Nice this busiest weekend of the Monaco Grand Prix-no small feat.

One hour into the search, Max is coming up empty-handed for hotels with his Australian assistant online. Ray mentions, "We were unable to book months in advance, and thought just staying up all night in and around the casino and race could work for us. The excitement would keep us awake. We can just catch up once onboard our cruise ship, early afternoon."

Max volunteers, "I'm game for staying up all night, if it means playing in the casino." Diana's expression does not indicate interest in this wild hair scheme. Without reservations and no room availability, we contemplate this crazy venture in the casino of Monte Carlo. The established playground of billionaires is beyond our means but for an overnight. Millionaires are commoners and can't seem to keep up the status symbols and paled in "being rich" by comparison.

I gaze out the train window at the sparkling Mediterranean Sea en route to Nice and reflect on the events of the preceding few hours. We are now riding along the coastal tracks from San Remo to Cannes. What was to be a smooth, relaxing express train ride to The French Riviera from Milan, turned into an upheaval of timing and circumstance that day. How did our paths cross into this harrowing experience for the Australians?

To our amazement, just thirty minutes outside of Nice a call came into Max saying, "We've secured two hotel rooms with views." Max's management team produces two rooms the busiest night of the year in Nice. Not a high-star hotel, but of course we'll be paying high-star rates. Max made dinner reservations at one of his familiar favorite restaurants.

Not even the threat of danger, no sleep, and juggling accommodations are going to spoil that evening for a respite from the escape. Astonishingly enough, in the delight of good company, we all laugh and joke. I again press my head against the window and focus on the glistening coastal sea view with twilight approaching as the train nears our arrival at the Nice, France terminal. I was focused on that sleek Silversea luxury cruise to relax over the next week.

Ray was groaning at the idea of an expensive night in Nice and preferred to grab a quick bite. However more importantly at that moment, I needed to eat and sleep and get in holiday mode, so that is when survival beats plans. Exhausted at this point, it took some major muster to work up the inertia. Besides, Max and Diana were so altogether engaging, there was no denying their graciousness.

Our room is bare bones simple at $375 a night in 2006. Less than what we could lose in the casino I stood to reason. We did however have a peek-a-boo view of the Mediterranean out on the terrace. It wasn't until we shower and walk nearly a mile to dinner with Max and Diana through a dark park along the Gold Coast, Cote D'Azur, that fear of the danger of the situation began to settle in.

My imagination races to the Albanians jumping out of the bushes and holding us hostage. We could have been followed and as far as the Albanians were concerned, we may be in cahoots with Max and Diana.

Max's energy level, particularly under the circumstances is contagious and while it all sounded exciting on the train, the evening blended into a calm in the simple chic restaurant we had to ourselves. Over dinner, Ray and Max compared skiing stories in their youth and Max shared their plans to buy a home in Chamonix, France.

The Aussies had three little ones under high school age, waiting at home in Australia. Their oldest son had the privilege to pursue his dream of being an Olympic skier and train in Chamonix. After dinner we returned through the dimly lit wooded park, with my guard up. We bid our goodnight, *au revoir* in the lobby of the high-rise hotel and rode up the elevator six stories to our room.

The exhaustion had put my anticipation for one of the biggest deals in my life aside. We ventured the expense after all; since this vacation is a combination celebration of our Anniversary and both of our Birthdays. These were privileged lifestyles beyond our means, but we ventured for a once-in-a-lifetime vacation. At six AM the next morning we awoke and made sure we weren't being followed by anyone Albanian looking, as we exited the hotel lobby. Whatever that was, I wondered. Dash the thought, for the sleek and chic of a luxury cruise is at hand.

Invigorated to stroll along the Cote D'Azur promenade, smell the sea and view the emptied streets of Nice, early morning after the Grand Prix revelers, we saw only one car on the Promenade des Anglaise, a sun-yellow Ferrari, of course. We must have been the only ones up that hour who hadn't celebrated with Cristal champagne all night.

Bravissimo! The big day to board our first-ever luxury cruise in Ville Franche Sur Mer, France, a picturesque definition of a charming town with three stops in Italy. The quaint little town is tucked in the crescent cove between Nice and Monte Carlo. I flash back on the port of Cary Grant's grandmother in *An Affair to Remember* with the monumental romance of that scene and era.

We have a few hours to explore the narrow, cobblestone alleyways and admire the picture postcard village. Bright red geraniums cascade over the window boxes everywhere as if waterfalls of red blooms poured from the balconies. Several blocks up the hill, I turn and stand to peer through the narrow shaft of daylight in between buildings and down the alley to a slice of the blue sea.

There the beauty floats in the quiet cove, The Silver Whisper. Seven days aboard ship visiting Jewels of The Mediterranean. Six-star service with room service any hour of the night and just about whatever your heart desires on a silver platter, complimentary. A vacation free from major decision-making. Three stops in Italy - Sicily, Sorrento, and Rome along with Barcelona, Spain, and the islands of Majorca and Malta.

The biggest decisions once onboard are which shore excursion to choose, what to eat, which restaurant to dine in, and what to wear from the walk-in closet with two formal evenings. I have my own cabin steward and staff numbers are nearly equal to passengers. Though it is my first six-star treatment, I instantly adapt to a life of nobility.

All worries on land are now behind us. No packing and unpacking, tour arrangements, or where to eat is a concern. My expectations are now raised like the sails going out to sea. The World of Italy and throughout the Mediterranean are at my doorstep. A whisper of discovery is in the air. I hear the seagulls calling...a life soaring above the waves.

Chapter 8

All Aboard Luxury Cruise

The Silversea cruising experience is exquisite, like having a butler on holiday without the personal intrusiveness of one. It is life-changing, if you haven't had a taste of the indulgent life on a five to six-star level. Based on the affluent vacation accommodations and gathering experiences of the discerning, Silversea was founded by a Roman family and The Group of Monaco, interested in more than what luxury and carte-blanche passage can bring. For a once in a lifetime experience and a promotion that made it more affordable, we thought such a heightened experience might send us to the moon.

Looking back, it was serendipitous for us to gain passage since I responded to an ad in the San Francisco Chronicle for Silversea Cruises where our cost of voyage was discounted by half since they were looking to fill the ship with passengers. We were already planning an Italian venture near those dates.

Italians have major maritime influence. The ships originated in Italy out of the finest materials featuring rosewood inlay cabins, initially built in Genoa by one of the world's leading shipbuilding companies, and, of course, skippered by Italian crews from Captains on down. They recruit world-class chefs from around the globe to run the galleys, and their cuisine is certainly Italian inspired. Seasonal and regional, the menus depend on the port of the day with the cuisine of the region.

Silversea is what ultra-luxury bestows, but not just in the embellishments. Italians and crew provide the unencumbered, relaxed feeling that quickly vanishes daily stresses from home. After lifting anchor, you soon feel transported, with the ability to see many countries in one comfortable journey. Such a cruise into foreign lands is tailored to provide a condensed slice of life through the ages and generations.

I dive into a retreat and indulgence from the routine. Waking up each morning as we approach the most romantic and exotic coastlines, we are transported from our everyday life and culture to changing our views of the world. Luxury Cruising is living in the New World while venturing into the Old World each day.

A little village along the French Riviera, Ville Franche Sur Mer is our due destination for this April 2004 launch. A cruise of the Mediterranean aboard a luxury line, The Silver Whisper awaits. Where six-star service is at your doorstep, *Jewels of The Mediterranean* is our gem studded itinerary. The Monaco Grand Prix in Monte Carlo is in full force this weekend. Merely a few coastal coves away from Ville Franche where the billionaires play.

In Monte Carlo, millionaires in the lower range now need not apply, as was evident even back in the 1980's on my first visit to the miniature and famous tax haven. Monaco is a country of less than a square mile and the lure began with the Casino. Even commoners are glamorously poised here.

Since it was near impossible to book a hotel room at this busiest Grand Prix time of year, Ray and I decided six months in advance, we'd wing it in Monte Carlo and stay up all night in the casino if necessary. After an intriguing couple days in Milano visiting major sights, we boarded a perilous train ride from Milano to Cannes as previously described in our escapades.

Silver Whisper, so aptly named, glides across the sea ever so gracefully. Listening to the hull cut through the weight of the vast waters and slicing winds with the hushed sound of a light splash and spray brings a soothing sound like therapy. The waves part and emanate radiating off the ship with white topped caps in concentric force.

The engaging and intriguing daily excursions offered by the onboard concierge, are as inspiring as a richly choreographed ballet. History, fine art, and culture dance at your feet and within steps of where the crew of the Silver Whisper drops anchor. The day is jam-packed with visiting recommended attractions, and we feel invigorated by the sea, the sun, and mankind's accomplishments throughout the ages where Western Europe is within your reach. With each daily passage, exotic, intriguing new locations are brought about, like so many curtain calls that keep the exhilaration. I'm inspired to live life to its fullest again and pursue the dreams longed for, both anticipated and realized. Our voyage motivates me to make bold changes, upon returning home.

Two years later, without a vacation, we leave home in San Francisco for our second Silversea cruise and a long-awaited Spring Tour 2006. "Iberia and Riviera Vistas" launches in Lisbon, Portugal. Lisbon is considered the San Francisco of Europe. We jet through Heathrow, London to Lisbon, for three days. Lisbon lies in the hills of Portugal and has all the architectural wonder of any cosmopolitan European city. Lisbon is often bypassed due to its distant location at the southwest corner of Portugal on the Atlantic Ocean and neighboring Spain.

Our flight to Lisbon, Portugal to start our Mediterranean Cruise was nearly without a glitch. Layovers in airports without airline waiting rooms or other luxury benefits can be stressful in Europe. Since a meal wasn't offered on the flight, when we arrived in London and with the time change, I was feeling faint for a lack of nourishment, oxygen, and sleep. In addition, Heathrow was overly crowded and bustling.

We step up to the Red-Carpet Room with our one-time pass, snubbed by the British receptionists who examined us as if our pass were counterfeit. After sixteen hours of flying time, I was in no mood to put up with their overly snooty discretion. I raised an Italian conniption fit in my exhausted state and they finally honored the darn thing.

A lovely surprise, Lisbon, and we spent three splendid days downtown walking through historic landmarks, squares; and peeked at window shopping. The likeness of Lisbon to San Francisco in geography and architecture is so striking that we felt right at home. The city provides cable cars for public transport, and they have a bridge nearly identical to the Golden Gate Bridge. Lisbon has many more traditional buildings from the 1800s architecture. The hilly terrain above the sea makes for breathtaking vistas.

From Lisbon, we begin ten days aboard the Mediterranean Riviera Cruise to ultimately land in Genoa, Italy. Aboard our second Silversea Cruise, we couldn't wait to travel again along the romantic coastal entrance to our destinations. The coastal beauty summons a dreamy feeling at sunrise as we glide through glistening waters, into the seaports.

My previous cruise stopped at most ports of call in Italy. This cruise has only two Italian destination ports. Visiting the ports in other countries makes for a good reminder as to why I love Italy so much more than other European countries. The day of our cruise departure, we summon a taxi to the port. Our driver was very offended when Ray said, gracias Senor, since *obrigado* is the Portuguese thank you. They are very proud of their heritage and this cab driver made sure Ray knew the distinction with several strongly emphasized *obrigados*, as we soon understand during our Portuguese travel. The Portuguese language is gentler and more romantic. I think of it as a combination of French and Spanish, or Franish. After three weeks in Brazil over New Year's in 1991-92, I was under the enticing influence of the Portuguese language.

As we sit in the boarding station to the cruise ship, I observe passengers trickle in. It soon becomes apparent that there are two different ships boarding at the same time. Our cruise is very formal with over half on board, British. The other ship is a Windstar Cruiser-smaller, for the more active, adventure sport sailing crowd, some bearing backpacks.

Having arrived nearly two hours early for embarkation gave me plenty of time to read and observe the passengers we will join. It is always an option to choose your fellow diners onboard Silversea, so I was scoping for fellow diners. The couple sitting next to us was deeply embedded in their reading. When others started arriving and seating space diminished, the young man next to me was forced move in closer.

At this time, he asked if we were boarding the Wind Star Cruise and he shared the following story: he and his wife were now taking their second cruise on board Windstar, complimentary, because their previous voyage to Greece had been interrupted by a ship malfunction.

Soon a family group of prominent Spaniards came in and raised the roof with their high-volume bantering. Mama Marquez, in her eighties, was escorted to a seat right next to me, and she had her entire brood of 13 adult children accompanying her. All sisters and brothers made this annual one-week holiday. Fortunately, the quietest two, Marisa and Hernando, sat next to me once the Wind Cruise passengers. The others couldn't sit still and kept on echoing throughout the terminal. All thirteen siblings plan this 21st annual vacation together. Neither spouses nor children are allowed.

How marvelous, something I have dreamed about in my large family of seven kids, however when I suggested it, I was either ignored or put in my "are you kidding" place. Oh well, I believe the Marquez are doing it right. It's not often I know families that enjoy their in-laws.

Obviously, the in-laws of the Marquez family have never refused it, and if they did, were willing to forego the circumstances. I think it's healthy because, for most families, the in-laws are bored or bothered by another family's traditions and tend to feel left out even when present. No one can be closer in history than growing up as siblings.

Once onboard, the Marquez Clan is the major force in shaking things up aboard somewhat stiff Silversea guests. On the other hand, I do enjoy more the fact that with a mostly British, American, and Italian passenger list, one doesn't have to worry about annoying or unruly behavior during events or poolside. You're in close quarters with less than 300 passengers for ten days.

In other words, the partiers and good timers found each other real fast. Those couples looking for quiet romance would keep to themselves. Those too stiff or preoccupied to enjoy spontaneous socializing found themselves as well. And those too judgmental to mingle once they disapproved of your origin, political or social behavior, stood back.

Ray and I overall are nonjudgmental and tend to gravitate to the good timers because after all, on vacation, why be anything else? Once you're seated with people you don't enjoy and have been established by others as "not their type," we go our merry way with those who are more open-minded and receptive. The only "type" we avoid is unfriendly.

Once we walk the red carpet and climb the stairs to board the ship, we are greeted with a glass of champagne, a jazz ensemble, and a tastefully displayed table of hors d'oeuvres including caviar, pate, etc. The feeling gives me goosebumps for having arrived in the lap of luxury. As soon as we get our security passes, we're escorted to our room by our chambermaid, who functions like a butler as well.

Ray immediately starts unpacking and I'm out the door back to the reception area to savor this moment. Eating appetizers, feeling the champagne, and hearing the crooning of Frank Sinatra's "Under My Skin," a favorite serenade, puts me in that frame of mind so rarely achieved. With complete satisfaction under my skin and through my bones, the excitement finally sinks in, having finally arrived at our departure destination after days of uncomfortable travel and adjustment.

After fifteen minutes, I run back to our cabin wondering where Ray is as he is missing this special moment. The chambermaid, Gerta with an extremely concerned expression is outside the door to say, “Mrs. Evans, we’ve been looking for you!” Gerta looks like Uma Thurman.

Ray is sprawled on top of the bed with his nose bleeding profusely and surrounded by several bloodied towels. I’m very confused as to why no nurse or doctor has been summoned. “What on earth happened?” I wail. Ray calmly says, “Oh it’s nothing bad, I just bumped my nose on the closet hanger rail after raising up from the floor while unpacking my shoes.” He keeps saying, “it’s nothing-you go have a good time.” I’m thinking, how could he possibly do this with a good size walk-in closet?

Leave it to Ray - my “bull in the China closet.” Well, he made that vision stick in full form now as “the bull in the closet.” So, before we can even get to muster, the emergency drill, they’re paging the ship’s doctor. Instead of a doctor, Gerta arrives with another chambermaid, who insists she was a nurse in Argentina. Ray is starting to get a colorful eye, a shiner that is. I’m sure the nurse from Argentina will have the perfect solution. My fifteen minutes of heaven have quickly vanished.

I call the doctor’s office and the doctor is not very pleased to be disturbed already, upon just boarding ship. He does a little exam with light and probing. The good Polish doctor proceeds to tell us he should have it x-rayed here in Lisbon. I ask the good Polish doctor, “How does Portuguese medical service rate, compared to the U.S.?” (Already afraid of the answer) Ignoring my question he gruffly retorts, “You should go to the hospital.”

“Well, I said to Ray, let’s wait it out. If you can survive the pain, I’d rather not do anything since the doctor seems in question as to whether Ray’s nose is broken or not.” Ray has no trouble agreeing with me, since this is his wish. After all, why spoil a perfectly luxurious vacation at an unknown hospital in an unknown country. We’ll find out in Portuguese something we already know, and you can’t do much about a broken rhino.

This beaten by football tackles and ski accidents protrusion of a nose, may set itself right without a glitch. Another slight bend won't blemish the man.

I call the Cruise Director and say we're going to have to miss the muster. "Ray needs to stay lying on his back with ice for a while longer." Yippee for small blessings! Right off the bat this drill puts the fear of The Titanic in you, and we get to miss it. The passengers look like a bunch of penguins stuffed in orange life vests gathered around the safety crew near the emergency boats. I do not underestimate its importance; however, the whole drill is quite comical in appearance to me.

At the poolside a few hours later, there is no shortage of good timers on board, once the water volleyball games begin. For starters, The Kiwis as we named them, are two young raucous couples from New Zealand. The women love to stir the quips of sarcasm and cheer to keep things lively while hitting the ball about. For the Kiwis, it means lots of uninhibited pleasure with drinking from early morning till late night.

I have no idea how they kept this pace for ten days with just a few hours of sleep each night. They weren't that much younger than Ray and I and without the drinking, I was usually cabin bound by 10 PM to make the next morning's 8 AM port of call wake up and landing. I wanted full steam for soaking in each day's shore excursions to exciting new ports.

Regarding interesting passengers, one evening we sat between two opinionated and judgmental couples. It was fun sitting back and watching the sparks fly from a dowdy British matron and an outgoing D.C. Washingtonian, spar on who was the more formidable figure to the public in the British Line of Royalty between the Queen and late Princess Diana. Bring on the Queen's guard because it feels as if we're in the middle of a British/American mutiny if these two keep up the volume of their spat. I'm thinking, help get me out of here, since this is their idea of a fun vacation or relaxation.

I met the Sweet as Mint Juleps, Southern Belles of Tennessee, Suzanne, Sherry, and Jen, while waiting for our Italian dinner, dressed in formal attire for our second of three formal dinner nights. That is three formal nights of our ten-day cruise. With such outfitting, packing lightly is a challenge.

Suzanne and I exchanged greetings while outside on the bow of the ship gently cutting through waters, near dusk in the twilight. She is with her husband Lee, the ultimate Southern gentleman and her two girlfriends Sherry and Jen. "We're from Na-a-a-shville," Suzanne says with that endearingly familiar Southern drawl, and Jen pipes in "I'm from Meh-eh-eh-mphis and all we have is El-l-l-lvis." Immediately I like these unpretentious Southern gals. How unlikely for a husband and wife to travel accompanied by her two girlfriends. They resemble the best version of the Ya-Ya Sisterhood.

We sip our cocktails and divert to a cheese round the size of a basketball. The sun shone brightly in our eyes and the ship sliced through the water as easily as a sterling silver knife made especially for cutting through the wedding cake.

As I stood face to face with Suzanne, I noticed her eyes are a similar rare green/hazel shade as mine. It was a stand back and take notice moment, something I have never seen in anyone else's eyes, in all my 40-plus years, traveling halfway around the world and back again. Not only were they stunning green, but her eyes also smiled and sparkled. I comment to Suzanne. "So many eyes and yours are the first I've noticed to be the same shades of green. We-e-el-l-l…" That was the start of sisterhood as we strike up a conversation and feel a familiarity.

Suzanne is stunningly beautiful. Her friend Sherry is perfectly slender, coiffed with her Chanel-style hair and ensemble. Her makeup is flawless every day. Jen is a hoot with her gregarious, raspy alto voice and animated mannerisms. She loves to eat and smokes like no tomorrow. They all dress impeccably.

Lee, Suzanne's husband pulls out his perfect southern gentleman mannerisms. He's quiet, well-heeled with silver-white hair parted and combed with not a hair out of place. Lee deserves applause for allowing his wife to bring along her two girlfriends, with all their comfort needs and accouterment. They are as kind as they are attractive.

Of course, some of the women's comments, and Sherry herself, intimated that she deserves sainthood after living with a southern traditionalist all these years. Manly men love to dominate. Any married woman knows these struggles for control crop up in nearly every marriage. We dined at our own tables that night, and the following day we docked in Valencia, Spain and bumped into Suzanne and Lee in the middle of the city plaza. I tell Suzanne she looks like Joan Collins (most definitely) and Lee exclaims, "Oh no, she'll forever be your friend now."

The next time we ran into Suzanne and Lee on board, they asked us to join them for dinner, to which we delightfully agreed. It was the most entertaining foursome, these seemingly unlikely co-travelers, and we laughed so hard at some of their quick wit, we had one of the best evenings onboard the ship, with people-watching and spontaneous quips. We exchange contact information as Suzanne insists that we come visit Nashville, while we're on our trip to St. Louis in September to see the history and culture their city has to offer.

We kept in touch by email and arranged for one of the most glorious visits with friends we had ever attended, a catered dinner party and cruise reunion in our honor. The extraordinary décor featured live exotic fish at each table setting, swimming in their own little fishbowls. Suzanne and Lee were the most gracious of hosts we had encountered to date.

Portofino *Mi Piace,* I Like It

A Portrait of Portofino – May Day

Even with an overcast day and the spattering of rain, Portofino rises out of the sea like a sundrenched damsel in her castle with well coifed green hair in shades of olive, cypress, and pine. Rocky cliffs of limestone, jut out and show their interesting irregular faces climbing skyward.

The umbrella pine line the top ridge of the mountain like a dark green ruffle. Waters splash at the rocky seashore as if a lace trim. The large single pine above Castelli Brown stands like a prominent lady in the wind with her long hair blowing away from the neck in wispy waves.

Portofino is a small village that encompasses the narrow bay. In the background lies a palette of water-colored buildings lining the coastal waters. Some are homes, some Designer Boutiques and Cafes. The colors of the buildings are distinguishable from far at sea. This tradition of bright tasteful colors is truly Italian.

The yellow *cupola* and *campanile* bell tower of San Giorgio rises and rings this May Day to greet the warmth and voyagers at sea. It rings not just to tell the time but for what seemed unending chimes of joy and festivity on this most cherished day of spring and brings me joy returning to the memory of crowning the Blessed Mary, Mother of God in my youth.

May 1, May Day, is when Catholics all over the world celebrate Jesus' mother, Mary by a procession with a crown of flowers on her head. We honor her intercession for our prayer intentions. Just as a son or daughter loves an adoring mother, so do we honor Mary with such utter respect as being the first person to fully accept Jesus Christ into the world.

Sailboats, small fishing boats, and jet-set yachts anchor and mix in Portofino's port, where old fishermen dock their vessels next to yachts. Grey castle mansions seem to rise straight out of the same color stone as perfect camouflage. The main fortress tower in its sun-drenched terracotta welcomes visitors from its once imposing grey walls of war and warning in camouflage. Some are layered like cakes in colors from grey to yellow to orange. Homes climb the steep cliffs with bright and vivid colors, accented by trompe l'oeil hand painted around the windows, corners, and doors, pronouncing the brightly colorful way in which residents of Portofino live. They welcome seafarers in hues of yellow, ivory, orange, and terracotta.

Fishing villages where small fishing boats for two are afloat and empty in the shadowy waters, awaiting their next journey through the waters to bring fresh catch and celebrate the salty seawater. If I had to choose one of my favorite photographs from all Italian journeys, the prize has served as my screensaver on the computer. Two fishermen are rowing in a colorful dingy amidst yachts. One is hunched over, cleaning the freshly caught fish, and the other is rowing. The inside of the boat is bright turquoise, and the outside is trimmed in red with a white hull. Right next to them are many shiny new yachts anchored in Portofino Bay where two fishermen rest amongst yachts.

Portofino fishermen

We scaled the goat path up an incline to both the cathedral and castle atop Portofino. Here's where you find the picture postcard shots of the year. In between villas, you rise fifty feet and above to a panorama of the bay, sea, and villas. Even though you get the thick crowds like in Venice, it is worth every crowded step. Somehow, all the chaos blends into the Italian way, and everything even amidst unnerving commotion becomes simpatico. Travelers romance in the rhapsody of Portofino.

The Iberian Peninsula and The Mediterranean Cruise was taken in part to compare the likes of Italy and my love for all things Italian. It only reinforced my desire that even if I never visit another country, I will be satisfied to visit only Italy.

"You may have the universe, if I may have Italy," – Giuseppe Verdi

My sentiments exactly.

I overheard a fellow passenger on the ferry to *Camogli* say, "I'm that much more convinced now that I want to visit Italy only and can't wait to come back." *Camogli*, in the Liguria region is a gorgeous fishing village dotted with vividly colored buildings.

The brightly painted buildings started as a tradition for the fisherman, so that upon returning from sea after long journeys, they could recognize their home from afar when approaching the harbor. *Camogli* was founded for the wives of fishermen.

In comparison of our previous cruise stop the service in Portugal was lacking. The women did not want to serve a blonde American woman and made it apparent twice in Lisbon when I ordered for my husband as well. While Ray was away at the restroom, (his first act upon entering a café), I order a café espresso for Ray and sparkling water for myself. Two different times at two different cafés; the same results. His espresso arrives but no sparkling water for me.

Our last port stop is in Spain, where there are many beautiful cities, countryside, and *Costa del sol* settings. However, for me, none can compare with the sheer variety of architecture and art of the Italians. I observe Italians relate to Americans in a distinct personable and respectful manner.

Looking back, it was fateful I found an ad for half fare in the Chronicle for Silversea Cruises. Silversea will forever be the dream trip to Italy, where everything goes right, because of their impressive deluxe service and accommodations. There are times that cruising on Silversea is the perfect once in a lifetime venue to look forward to, especially when weary from home and work. It is the ultimate in relaxation - costly, however little add on fees.

In contrast to Silversea travels, the memories of my own planning lead me back to desired destinations on land with unexpected ventures and journeys left up to spontaneity connecting with Italians. The spontaneous will hold some of the brightest memories because of the serendipitous nature of meeting Italians and engaging in their traditions, or exploring with fellow travelers, the wonder of wanderlust. When you are on your own itinerary, there is ample opportunity to embrace the generous Italian nature, by going on the fly as signs from the Divine, so vibrant in the lives of Italians.

Camogli is Sanctity

There is a coastal hillside-hugging town along the Italian Riviera that is so sublime I shed a tear for joy upon approach. The dream destination of Camogli and San Fruttuoso is within The National Trust of Italy or FAI, Fondo per l'Ambiente Italiano, Italy's conservation program of historic interest and beauty established in recent history--1975. A tour boat transports you to this day excursion.

Camogli and San Fruttuoso did not disappoint.

The afternoon rays of the sun broke through for our tour to Camogli and San Fruttso.

The coastal town of Camogli sits on hillsides so steep that boat access is the only practical means of arrival. While approaching this less-discovered gem, docking the large boat required navigating through the marina past the protruding jetties of Camogli, and fishing village centuries old.

Camogli is simply and merely idyllic and takes its meaning from *la moglie*, wife. Her tall buildings shoot straight out of the mountain and are painted in bright splashes of color illuminating the village like gemstones. The rocky promontory at one point makes for a dramatic visage.

Many fisherman's wives have resided here thru the centuries. Their homes are painted in bright stand out colors, so the fishermen could recognize their own homes while approaching land from afar. After a long journey, these vivid and distinguishable colors which made them easy to identify, were a sight for sore eyes. You will find this a custom in numerous coastal and island towns of Italy.

Some homeowners have gone so far as to distinguish their flat on a building by painting each floor contrasting colors. For instance, a terracotta ground floor with a burnt yellow second floor and a crimson top floor all on the exterior of the same building in broad stokes of vivid color.

In 2018 Silversea was bought by Royal Caribbean. The Silversea has a fleet of twelve smaller ships, so if you want a similar experience to mine, book the original smaller ships. The cruise experience is a wonderful way to travel from one country or continent to another and preview locations, if you'd like to return, since life gives us so precious little time to explore and travel sites around the world.

Chapter 9

Bullish on Torino, Turin

We are at the end of our Silversea cruise and full of melancholy as we depart the Silver Cloud, so aptly named this overcast morning, boohoo. After ten glorious days, we must say goodbye in Genoa. Our shipmaster Nigel's morning broadcast in his most proper sing-song English accent, "Go-o- o-od (lilting upward) Morning, it's another Glo-o-o-rious Day" resounded throughout the entire ship in every suite as a wake-up call to port. His announcement, like clockwork, was a cock a doodle doo at 8 AM.

We disembark in our final port of Genoa to pick up a rental car for our destination Torino. Our taxi driver spoke no English and was unsure of which one to go to in the city. After numerous references to our Italian dictionary, we figured that he figured it out. The most persistent female agent at the rental car is insisting we take out extra insurance built into the charges. Ray is diplomatically trying to get out of these charges, in his kind assuring manner, forgetting that in Italy, you need to raise a raucous.

I'm letting him be the man in charge here, trying very hard not to jump into the mix. Every time Ray sees me starting to get upset, he says, "Now don't get your Italian up." In the meantime, three other customers have come and gone. Another customer says he doesn't want the insurance, very firmly right off the bat, and his wish is quickly honored.

After 30 minutes, I'm at my boiling point. Terse and hot-blooded is customarily Italian for getting your point across and perfectly acceptable if you insist with confidence. Ray, just let 'em have it, saying to myself, while I do my deep breathing to keep from interrupting. I'm thinking here it comes, one place I need to let it fly. "These are not the charges we accepted when I booked this car over the internet," I firmly exclaim. The woman agent finally agreed five minutes later, in patronizing manner. After that ordeal, we're off, forgetting to check the car for dings.

About an hour later into our drive and at our first pit stop called AGIP auto grill, we run in starving. If you're not familiar with these Euro pit stop gas stations/deli/gift/drugstores, it's rather amazing to find all this right off the autostrada. Most have a restaurant as well, and some are even floating on a bridge over the highway. I bought Ray reading glasses, eyeglasses being another Italian invention.

I run to the glass deli and select a prosciutto sandwich, *panino,* and a piece of pizza for Ray. As I return to the car, I take a bite and gag on the amount of fat in the meat. The sandwich is so heavy in fat that it looks like the kind of raw pork fat I could get sick from. Ray's complaining that why I would pick pizza for him, something so messy to eat while driving. I'm ticked off now since it is his favorite food. I told Ray, I'm going back in to exchange the *panino* because I'm too hungry to drive on and forget about it.

Back into AGIP at the counter, I explained the problem in broken Italian showing the prosciutto fat with only tiny marble streaks of prosciutto meat in the sandwich. She takes it back to the prep chef/manager who proceeds to shake his head no. I knew where this was going. I looked back at him and gave him the old Italian hand gesture with the fingertips held together under the chin, followed by the arm thrown out at the intended receiver shouting, "**You** can eat this *il stupido*, Italian." There with my Italian temper out, like a criminal, escaped and on the loose. The man sitting on the stool at the counter next to me looked absolutely dumbfounded. The counter girl was blank. I raced out to the car and didn't even care if the Mafia was now after me.

I blew a fuse and then my cool because after six-star treatment on the cruise, it was hard to take the torment at the rental car agency along with starving without an edible sandwich all in one morning. My heart is racing as I feel my pulse. I return to announce this debacle and Ray announces, "There's a good size ding on the passenger rear fender." I get out and race to the back of the car, and there it is. Now we know why the agent was insisting we get the extra insurance. The damage had been hidden amongst closely double-parked cars along the busy *strada.*

For the entire journey Ray and I are trying to figure out how to get the dent out without being noticed. Ray is already figuring we'll stop at an auto shop in Milan, the city of our departure. So fine, we'll forget about it the rest of the trip…or not.

From the Silversea ship's dock in Genoa, we head for the city of Torino in the Piedmont Region. Ray put his Mario Andretti driving skills into action for a few hours and got his land legs back. Getting our bearings on the *autostrada*, once you put yourself in the frame of mind as an Italian race car driver, the intimidation vanishes, and it seems like a normal, everyday mode of getting around. By late afternoon we are in Torino and arrive at Le Meriden Hotel, the famed former Fiat factory.

Torino, Turin, just hosted the 2006 Winter Olympic Games two months prior. "Passion Lives Here" was the slogan. The hotel, Le Meridien hosted The Olympic Committee and was transformed from a former Fiat Factory into both a five- and four-star hotel by a famous modern architect named Piano. The open-air lobby is ultimate modern and striking in wood and steel accents. Each door is framed solid hardwood. Even the walls of our room are adorned in wood.

The Receptionist had such a sharp, short clean haircut, I asked where her hair was done. Tired of my growing out stages and ready for a short fresh Euro look to manage a long, hot summer ahead in Palm Desert.

Valentina mentioned a salon close to downtown and was kind enough to call her hairdresser to see about squeezing me in the next couple of days.

Three phone calls later, Valentina was unable to book her hairdresser, and recommended a salon right here in the same building. Alongside all the shops, mostly for young of the Olympic age genre, she suggested Opera Salon is a good salon knowing a friend who is happy with them.

In the former factory, giant halls are now filled with the shops of a shopping mall. Blocks of boutiques and cafes that seem to run for miles. Certainly, the largest mall I have ever seen. The main outside entrance has escalators a high-tech glass escalating elevator, climbing alongside the escalator.

Pedestrian Bridges extend out over a railway track on the other side of the mall for half a mile to apartments that I suppose provided Olympian housing. The bridge joins the mall to the housing. A giant red arch, a modern sculpture, extends over the end of the bridge.

Beyond the arch, from several stories high you can see in the distance, the modern sail-like shaped building that held the figure skating competition. Just in front of it was a smaller building and next to that is now a large exhibition center and former arena.

The hotel has an enormous glass-walled atrium garden that flourishes with plants up to five feet high within a giant courtyard on Floor 0 as the Italians call it, what we know as 1st floor. On the roof you will find a racetrack that once tested Fiat cars and a large glass dome room for special meetings. In addition, there is an extraordinary art gallery in the building.

I rushed over that late afternoon to the salon and got in with the manager/owner Stephano for the following day. I could tell by the manner of the customer before me, Stephano was a top-notch precision hair cutter.

You see, the last three times I had been to Europe I went with the idea of getting a hairstyle. Reason? European salons, particularly in Italy require their hairdressers to attend three years of training. They are particularly skilled with razors. Since my hair is Italian, so naturally thick, and curly, it takes some severe thinning and blunt edge cutting to look good and last without going on the frizz. Italian professionals know what it takes for taming and shaping thick hair.

Stephano is extremely delicate with his technique and so fastidious, that he had to assist one of his trainees in the middle of my cut to get the look he was after on the young man next to me. All the while since he understood no English, we communicated with hands and pictures as to my desired hairstyle. A picture is worth a thousand words because it is the best cut and style I have ever had.

His charming assistant blew dry my hair with her stash of 5 brushes and half an hour of diligence. Astonishing! My new, slightly punked-out hip hairdo to look younger and feel cooler for the summer. Ray liked it so well, we did the equivalent of a photo shoot, at all angles in the hotel lobby to my embarrassment. I want to take it to my hairdresser back home to replicate it.

Taurini are the founding fathers of *Torino* - the bull, the tribe along the Po River valley-- hence the city's symbol is The Bull. Torino also was the first capital of Italy.

Taking a bus downtown was a language challenge with the driver. Where there is an advantage to few tourists comes the fact that most are not able to communicate a minimal amount of English. Turin has been an organized blue collar workforce town with all the *macchina,* auto factories in place--Fiat, Alfa, etc.

We were deposited by the bus driver after changing buses to find a driver that at least understood as Americans we wanted to go to the historical sites of the Piazza Castello. We were gracefully deposited at the nearest access and wandered through blocks of what seemed miles of portico covered pedestrian walkways, each beautifully standing over marble and granite walkways. Many were covered by the amazing architectural groin ceilings. Groin appears like a cardinal's cap and is very difficult to achieve in wood framing.

We meandered with no map for the "I don't know why" reason, with Ray's meandering fashion, that is, and stumbled on some ancient excavations in progress. Major portions of a Roman Theatre were on one side of the street and some equally ancient building bites on the other side. I say bites because sometimes all that's left is what appears to be stones or bricks as if dinosaur bites were taken out of them from time's unforgiving erosion - not a reference to dating back to the prehistoric age.

The ruins are heavily gated and fenced with ten feet high dark, wrought iron posts. Several archeologists are standing and digging through recently broken dirt. Without knowing the significance, the cathedral and giant halls held, I knew with all the school children swarming that historical interest is here even for Turin's own.

Ray was in no mood to go inside any museum displays after visiting so many. We continued through several blocks of ancient history, absorbing the surroundings and envisioning what events may have taken place in these halls and theatres.

When we returned to the hotel, I found out that within the San Giovanni Battista Church's walls was The Holy Shroud, housed there since the 1500s. The imprint of Christ's face and body on the linen shroud that was swaddled around him like a bandage is still controversial, yet highly regarded as authentic by Roman Catholics.

I was surprised by the magnitude of monumental buildings here in Turin, for it has been bypassed through the years due to its place as a working-class society. That doesn't make Turin any less important for history and events. I believe it is most likely that because there were no royalty and grandiose affairs at the time of the Renaissance and until recently it has gone undiscovered and overlooked by most travelers. Like our obsession with only rich and famous lives.

Travel becomes that much more attractive without having to hear other Americans complaining and the romantic nature of the Italian dialect even without understanding.

Being away from the beaten path keeps you feeling removed from your world, a true escape. There is no sense of romance in travel to me if I'm not feeling far away from anything ordinary in my own culture and daily life. From anything as simple as foreign mannerisms to astonishing ancient monuments.

We jumped on another bus to get close to the shopping and train station. With shops, cafes, and boutiques, we ducked into a little café right across from The University. There in this dark wood, dimly lit café that smelled of books and studying. Not the kind of intellectual studying for university classes one expects. I'm reminded of the late-night crammers I knew and practiced so often in my college years.

The extremely polite bartender/university student gave a warm and welcoming smile. He even went so far as to draw a spectacled happy face in the steamed, frothy cream of my latte. This adorable young man also gave us a petit cup sample of a dark chocolate syrup drink --*bicerin*. Luscious, as a chocoholic. Like a quick fix, shooting it straight into the vein in liquid form. Affogato is another mouthwatering beverage. Gelato "drowned in" hot espresso.

Not until we left had I noticed the University across the street and the reason so many young university students understood and spoke English well here. Also, they were fascinated by us as Americans since the recent Olympics. Torino is rather new to tourism and more an industrial city over the last two centuries. With all the University students around, the atmosphere was charged with energy and enthusiasm.

Brilliantly displayed within the giant pillared porticos of Torino are the storefronts that date back to the 1800s with all wood and curved glass windows. Loaded with artistically arranged confections like nothing seen here in the U.S. Talk about eye candy!

The following morning, we headed to the City Center Piazza where the famous Bull Café has welcomed patrons for over a century, since 1903. I could sense the significance of the elegant décor that accentuated this historical café and bar paneled in dark wood and a spiral staircase. The coffee bar was two deep in business suits. More of a jolt than a double espresso, there's nothing better to jump start the day than a cafe loaded with dashing Italian businessmen, first thing in the morning.

Window shopping across the piazza we came upon a window showing a beautiful men's jacket, Ray admired. Of course, the price was restrictive, and a kindly older gentleman began translating the meaning of the apparel names when he overheard our stumbling. When we complimented him on his thoughtfulness, he asked where we were headed next. After mentioning Albano Terme, he insisted we should have lunch in his "Bella" hometown about an hour's drive outside of Torino and in the hills. He gave us specific directions to Montechiaro near Asti, and we thanked him profusely.

Chapter 10

Reflections of Venezia and Magic in Montecchio

Afloat on land and sea. Afloat in the air. Afloat in glory. Venice is a state of mind where disguise and entertainment mesmerize. The city's nature is a buoy to the spirit where romance and intrigue abound. When you escape the crowds down a quiet shaded alley, Venice is a place to linger. Stand over a bridge and see the ebb of the boats down the narrow canals. I have a bittersweet relationship with this one-of-a-kind city of canals. A stage full of contrast.

Venice is a cornucopia brimming over with artistic fruit. Even still, I avoided Venice for nearly 15 years from a previous visit due to the swarms of visitors. Restaurant waiters waving menus in my face attempting to lure me in or claiming tips before offering change overshadowed the romance along with a vague feeling of being taken. Memories of a visit with an ex-husband faded.

Eventually, the fantasy aspect of Venice in all its beauty took hold again. The islands of Murano and Burano, just a short boat ride away are captivating and provide an authentic measure of how true Venetians live.

Quiet little waterways where boldly splashed houses sit side by side. So vivid and varied in color, it's as if I've opened a box of bright crayons.

Murano is where all glassmaking was moved because the fear of fire in Venice could be devastating. After a private taxi from my hotel to the Glass Factory and Showcase, I toured the glassmaking furnaces and marveled at the talent of blowing shapes from the end of a long tube. I purchased modern water glasses square with rounded corners that were very useful rather than the elaborate baroque looking majority of treasures in the showroom.

While awaiting the ferry to continue to the island of Burano where ornate hand-woven lace is crocheted, I happened upon an empty alleyway to see through darkened windows, glassblowers in front of their fiery furnaces. There once again the careful artisans stretch and mold glass shapes by blowing air through the long pipes with the glass on end. Torches shaped and reshaped figures, creatures, etc. at this point.

Through time the disguise and beauty of Venice still lure. I am ready to see the romantic side again with Ray, as he had never been. The land of the fanciful, fabled winged lion. Otherwise known as a gryphon. Only in Venezia could lions' fly. Why? Because Venezia carries the mystique of fantasy in her waters as the only surviving city of canals in Italy. Grand palazzos, masquerades, and charades of entertainment belong to her.

We set out to Venice by way of Abano Terme, west in the Veneto region and a spa town loaded with Germans. I couldn't wait to get back to sharing space with Italians. We boarded an early train at 8 AM through Padua packed with school classroom students: one group of third graders, the other 6th grade. The innocence in their faces and sweet gestures of friendship are heartwarming. I can feel a huge difference to the demeanor of American children. What pleasant memories of innocent times from these beautiful Italian *bambini*.

We arrived in Venezia by 9:30 AM and at the fashionable café bar even at the train, we wind all the way through the serpentine Venetian

Grand Canal. The waterbus is loaded with passengers, packed like sardines as the old expression goes.

I was surprised by my gusto to click picture after picture of palazzos, boats, bridges, corridors, and characters down water alleyways even after fourteen years passed. I feel perplexed by the paradox of Venice and my restrained desire to return to the very nature of overcrowded waterways and piazzas.

A pull in my heart has led me back to this most romanticized of cities. Perhaps Venezia would reveal what is under the mask of the evasive creature, and what she wears for me this time. Is it the waterways alone that draw tens of millions here or is it something beyond canals providing mystique? The fascinating, mysterious qualities resemble murky waters. Perhaps I missed something entirely about her demeanor before.

Venice is a paradox for the romantic. This dichotomy is exaggerated even more since it is difficult to feel romantic in a bustle of people. Unless of course, you venture to the islands of Murano or Burano or duck into a hidden alleyway. In Venice, it is easy to imagine stealing away around a maze of narrow, dark, and damp alleyways, as a cool, quiet respite.

Now adrift on the Grand Canal a calm comes over me even on this overcrowded *vaporetto,* passenger boat. My mind drifts into thoughts of how so many palazzos and civilizations have survived this anomaly of a city. We saw a lively farmers market that stretched a block along the narrow sidewalk lining the Grand Canal.

The Rialto Market, a giant open-air market held fresh fish of every kind. Tables and stands of fruit and vegetables stacked and displayed like precious gems of every color unloaded and loaded at the end of the day. Lively bartering took place with merchants and customers, arms and bags waving about.

We saw *batelli,* boats of all styles and sizes. Boats with sandbags, boats with cargo, water taxis for two to four, gondolas lined side by side in rows of ten or fifteen, *vaporettos* loaded like sardines, boats for trash removal and many little private transport boats. How they all motored about without incident is as fascinating as how Italians don't crash more in their *machina*, cars on the streets. Over nearly a month's time I did not see one crash. Nor have I ever on any visit. As to my little episodes with the car - more later.

To feel modern living mixed with Old World tradition, gives life a greater sense of purpose in time. There is no more apparent mix of Old World with New World than seeing a gondolier with cell phone to ear, firmly holding his rowing stance and busily chatting on his cell phone. My mind wanders back to the glorious era of Venetian Masquerade Balls with a few costumed passengers aboard the next traditional gondola passing.

After drifting and stopping on the *vaporetto*, loading, and unloading passengers, crisscrossing the canal at each of about fifteen stops, our fantasy amusement ride ran about three quarters of an hour. We landed at the end of the canal near San Marco Piazza. Winding all the way down the serpentine Grand Canal we were most surprised to see the Harry's sign right in front of us while disembarking from the ferry.

The famed Harry's American Bar which I'd read about, heard, and pictured for at least twenty years is the only American business like an establishment, even to Venetians. Harry's literally lay at our feet in this tiny little alleyway bar. The bar is no bigger than our living room with an upstairs dining and view floor. It took me by such surprise in this lounging, living room space.

We proceed as the first early bird customers at 10 AM to be greeted by a most congenial bartender who served us up some 7 Euro espressos at the bar, about $10 each. Oh well, what lengths one will go, to say I've been there and done that. We figured a return for lunch most likely would have run over $100 to sit, see, and be seen.

With the bump of congestion in the train station and on the waterways, once on land and wandering through alleys, I felt surprisingly free of cramped space. After our first stop and ducking into Harry's Bar for our wake-up espresso, we only ran into an occasional busy intersection or piazza.

As I meandered into an art gallery the size of a corner closet, a friendly face appeared. I found a *bellissima* painting of a gondolier in this *piccolo* art gallery and found my eyes fixated on it. I purchased it in no greater than 3 minutes. The lovely gallery dealer was comparing to another watercolor of buildings in bright vivid colors which I also admired. However, the water seemed to move in the light on this one and the perspective spoke more of a story to me. Back home I found the perfect antique gold leaf picture frame for my painting of a lone gondolier silhouetted down a narrow canal, approaching a lacelike detailed, balustrade bridge. As I gaze at the watercolor the colors of the waters glisten in golden sunlight and the greenish-grey shadows scallop beneath the row and gondola. A hazy bright light glistens above the bridge where day tries to break thru the barriers of the two standing buildings.

Also, I pulled out my little brown half sphere leather purse, found in a leather shop with very gorgeous gloves, belts, jackets, etc. The shopkeeper was so engaging, he even punched a couple of holes in the purse strap so that it sat more comfortably and closer under my arm. A purse for a very tall person. Such an extremely long strap would otherwise hang below my hip.

Moving on through San Marco Square, we stood and soaked in the sun and water's edge. More pigeons than people perched at ten in the morning, and we shared taking photographs with a young romantic couple. As the most famous Piazza of Italy, you can feel the presence of millions passing by. The Duomo of the Basilica stands as a landmark from anywhere in Venice. The combination of Byzantine, Romanesque, Gothic, and Arabic make it peculiarly unique. A history of trade for centuries as the major center of Europe.

Today, again as a reminder of my previous visit, a bride in a blinding, crisp white gown beautifies the grayness of San Marco Square like a dove amongst pigeons. She tiptoes to pose for the photographer and her groom. How heavenly to see a bride covered in pure white and yards of fabric dance across the Piazza while her tulle veil wisps through the air like clouds moving across the sky on a gentle breeze.

In contrast, I remember a dismal picture of winter in an old Time magazine, with narrow planks two feet above the standing water on the often-flooded piazza. People precariously walk these narrow pieces of wood. One must become adept like a balance beam gymnast to live here I suppose, and face this weather dilemma that repeats itself.

Strolling further through some shops no larger than a walk-in closet, I found a menagerie of masks and all things Venetian brimming over from ceiling to floor. Hundreds of masks hung from the low ceiling on ribbons as in a shroud around his counter. I could feel eyes peering out from under a mask and the owner with kind eyes, Giorgio pops out. I proceeded to buy six gifts extraordinaire of mask pins and Murano *millefiori* beads, meaning thousands of flowers. Beads of Venetian glass that have a distinct daisy design within. The shop owner patiently pulled out gorgeous scrollwork gift bags for every pin gift and thanked me with those very kind eyes.

I felt a special moment when the shop owner/artist gave me the gift of himself through a piece of his culture, art, and heart. It was irresistible to have Ray take a picture of Giorgio in his mask menagerie shop the size of a closet.

These works of art save a page of memory in my life to revisit at home whenever I wish. Mementos I can wear or display make me happy. They will jog my memory when age fogs it. Even with the over-inflated Euro to the undervalued dollar which rose from $1.18 to $1.32 in just three weeks, I feel that the deflation of the dollar against the Euro is a mere pittance to pay for the special experience an Italian shop owner shares. Many offer a story about a piece of jewelry or leather and offer their character. Giorgio of the masquerade shop certainly did.

I also bought clear glass multicolored trays known as *Artistico Vetro* or Artistic Glass. Here in Giorgio's treasure trove. From the island of Murano such famous glass has been sculpted for centuries. One little square tray is made of a dozen little one-inch squares of various colored glass. Ruby, aqua, royal, green and sun colors. Another tray was in three shades of watery blue with a few *fiore,* flowers dotting the frame.

We were now starved for a quick bite on the go since after all we have is but one day in Venice. The *bacari* are lively little wine bars serving *cicchetti,* or small snacks. With the crowds bearing down in the alleys outside, we ducked into a *bacaro*, and deli another closet size L shape. Obviously, space is prohibitive on the island. Just the ticket for a quick bite. We ordered pieces of pizza. *Bacari* are a great way to save money in pricey cities and better still, rub elbows with locals on the go. All the nibbles are nummy.

I want to grab all the gusto I can in one day and go back to the spa and springs swimming pool to diffuse. So of course, never enough pizza. *Niente basta* pizza. Half a block down in eyesight while standing at the outside bar eating, a pair of masked live mannequins were motioning. There is something mischievous about these allegorical masks, wicked in expression. They wear flowing metallic robes, one in silver, and one in gold with matching masks.

We're familiar with moving mannequins in San Francisco's Union Square who are ready to be photographed with the next subject. They hope for a mere euro or more in the collection basket. I'd been exhausted from giving handouts by then, so I took Ray's picture eating pizza from a distance with the mannequins in the background luring other customers.

Now nearing the *stanca*, tired time with shops closing for the obligatory naps from 2-5 PM we do our meandering thru corridors and narrow dark alleyways where locals live. Some alleys are no more than 4-5 feet wide, dark, damp and depleted of any sunlight amongst tall buildings. This is the romantic quiet side of Venice everyone yearns for once the escape is found outside of tourists.

One glissade across the water and chasses through the stone alleyways particularly when finding a small off-the-beaten-path, with residents. We walked behind a diminutive old lady carrying her fresh market sack, probably from the famous Rialto Market. She turns to the door and steps up her stairwell.

My intuition on our walk back toward the train station landed us right in front of a cathedral housing the exhibit of some of Leonardo DaVinci's greatest inventions. We arrived at the door of San Giovanni by a sign from the Divine for an exhibit of many prototype machines. Artisans outside of Firenze, Florence have crafted sketches for over thirty years to make exhibits tour internationally. Puzzling is the fact that no one else on this beautiful spring afternoon is in the exhibit. Another sign from above. No lines or crowds, just a small banner above the entry.

Each of more than thirty models is more fascinating than the next since many are unrelated in the field. The intrigue of one man inventing and creating so many engineering feats from military to mechanics is jaw dropping. From a double-hulled ship to suspension bridges to ammunition, lighting, time measurement, bicycles not to mention wings of flight most of us know. All these inventions gathered in one place are astounding to see, particularly under the circumstances. What lies in the brainpower of one genius so ahead of his time? A true genius, both a controversial and misunderstood Renaissance Man. The Da Vinci Exhibit is a marvel.

The truth about Leonardo is far more intriguing than any of these theories sprung from speculation on one of his Masterpiece Paintings. Leonardo the Inventor, Engineer, Artist, and Anatomist seems so highly evolved beyond man today that I wonder what his peers and the public thought of him. The question of his personal life and habits arises as contrary to the religion he served. In each of these fields, he excelled light years beyond those of his day. The discoveries and truths that one man shared to improve the lifestyle and comforts of mankind are such a marvel to me, that more exposure to the real man is a must to inspire generations to come.

Upon our return near the train station, we wanted one more go of Venice and in the late afternoon, we discovered a quiet park for refuge on the other side of the canal, not far from the huge parking center where land lovers disembark. With the park in eyeshot, we stride over the bridge and to the nice respite in a small park.

Now Ray needs more Euro, so when asking a shopkeeper where the nearest bank ATM is, she said "you can go this'a way, or you can go that'a way". I asked, "Which is closer?" She retorted, "Either way'a you'll run into one in a few *minuti*". Haaah, "Grazie for the specifics" I reply. Perfectly understandable and distinctive directions in Italianism. We found a bank about ten minutes later. I am waylaid by another wandering musician whose rendition of Hayden on the violin is mesmerizing.

The violinist, sounded a virtuoso, playing in the shadow of a chapel on the little piazza, and gathered an audience admiring his tender sound. "Enough", says Ray, the man on the mission is off to the bank. "Ray, I see some *carabinieri,* police", standing outside that building.

Carabinieri is a good indication either an office of a public official or a bank is present. I asked the handsome police in black with red ribbon striped, tuxedo style pants, if I could take their picture. In true Venetian form without any pause, the two nodded but without distraction.

The overbearing crowds must give cause to be nonchalant compared to the previously surprised and happy subjects of my camera. Anyway, whether they liked it or not I snapped my photo while they continued their conversation facing one another. Ray retrieved the cash spit out by the ATM. The procedure always took at least two tries, sometimes two cards because it didn't like the first one or was difficult to understand -chalk it up as automated Italianism.

Carabinieri are some of the finest specimens of men, even Italian men. Chiseled features like the marble sculptures that adorn every *piazza* and *strada.* Because there are so many strikingly handsome men in Italy it appears they pick some of the best looking for police work. Ray no doubt was getting annoyed by my comments of all the gorgeous men, but I say to sisters who enjoy aesthetic beauty, one can't help but exclaim or at least raise your eyebrows. Testosterone oozes from the Italian Machismo.

Besides, Ray bears witness to the Kiwi, New Zealander women who performed scandalous acts on the cruise a few days prior. Lucia ripped the chef's shirt off, as a part of her dance on the lounge floor, never mind her husband standing there at the bar. The other Kiwi, Katrina had put the short bald waiter's head in her hands with a thrust to her bosom and threw back a laugh.

We make a last stop visit to the Rialto Bridge where a most charming and well-traveled British couple were taking pictures of each other. I volunteered Ray, the better photographer, to get a shot of them both and they obliged with an exchange of picture taking so we, too would have a shared moment in this legendary locale. We also exchanged stories about lovely Bath, the countryside garden town being our favorite place in England to visit. Bath is home to one of the best-preserved Roman Baths in the world for viewing only.

Off to the Venice train station with 45 *minuti* to departure. I pondered this beguiling and bewitching city outside on the steps that ran right down into the Grand Canal. A professional photographer stood right next to me with her enormous telephoto lens snapping this'a way and that'a way. I asked her if she was on an assignment, and she replied for a Vancouver Periodical.

I consider how exciting it must feel to have your work take you to the most sought-after destinations in the world. Now I prefer a quieter mode of work and vacation. While writing my book, I don't feel any deadlines or need to be doing exacts in any given situation. The only pressures now are self-inflicted and still hear my father's voice in the background saying, "Do something!" That's plenty enough combined with Catholic guilt.

Back to Abano Terme by way of Padua and Montegrotto Abano has merged with Montegrotto train station. I was praying that the Germans had an evacuation of the town so I could enjoy our second night with more Italians. I'm not getting much material here without observing Italians. The sign at the entrance of town reads, "Welcome, please avoid disturbing noises." I'm hoping while I was away, they hung a sign saying, "Welcome Italians and warm, fun-loving people". I'm taking liberty here and appreciate Europeans can live without the need to be politically correct.

When we arrived back at the Montegrotto Train Station, workmen were finishing off a brand-new iron and glass canopy entry in front of a newly remodeled station. The canopy is as grand as a modern Parisian hotel entry, welcoming to the remote little village. We certainly made our Venetian day the most event-packed, sightseeing of the entire trip.

On September 8, 2006, as if resurrected from the sea's floor, a vision of Michelangelo's Pieta hovered over the Grand Canal. In a gliding manner like a ballet dancer's glissade across the stage, an extraordinary sculpture is paraded on an open boat through the Grand Canal of Venice. The life-size Carrera white marble sculpture entitled "Michael Angel's –The Universal Pieta" is an exact replica of The Pieta in St. Peter's Basilica, Vatican. There is only one addition. The monument bears the stars and stripes flag of America, sculpted, unfurled, and draped under the body of Christ. The colors of the flag, boldly unfold red, white, and blue in all its glory and in boldly visible against the virgin white marble.

A most compassionate sculptor in Italy, offered a tribute befitting a king to the unbearable loss suffered by families from 9/11. The symbol represents the Virgin Mary's ultimate sacrifice with the loss of her only son portrayed in one of man's finest art forms. So too with the draping of the flag on this icon of Italian Art, reflects the loss of purity and loss of American lives in all wars as freedom fighters.

Such devotion in honor and loyalty to America, I believe in Italy is shown nowhere else on earth. They lived with the possibility of their country being run into fascism. For this I salute Italia, I feel at home. Beyond all theatrics in government and behavior, Italian emotion and purity of heart beat a pulse close to my heart. For all their disguises, today Venice wears no mask or costume. As I write these words, today is Halloween.

Magical Montecchio

Our next day is a stop in Montecchio Maggiore, home to the famed Montecchios or Montagues as we know in English. Where legendary Romeo and Juliet met and made their marriage in heaven, lies Montecchio Maggiore. The more likely authentic place of their origins, not just the famed little balcony room in the Verona location. Blessed by magic in Montecchio, the town is right off the autostrada between Vicenza and Verona where this little-known castle and fortress stands mightily atop the hill.

The Castle, *Castello* Montecchio is captivating and rises so high above the Medieval Town it feels like we're winding our way to the heavens. Romeo's ancestry reigned here. My good fortune is in discovering this best kept secret. The castle directions are so inconspicuous, it took us three times driving around town to find the signs and narrow winding roadway to the crest, with the fortress standing mightily atop the hill.

Most think of Juliet's balcony in Verona as the only sight to romanticize and ponder the legendary love story above all other love stories and send love letters to a staff of women who respond daily.

After heated deliberation with Ray expressing not going at all, my Italian flared up as I had my heart set on seeing this less discovered location and dug my heels in to visit the castle. He finally conceded to finding our way through town to take an arbitrary road amongst many and instinctually turn up the hill. With about ten minutes of serpentine climbing in the car, we passed vineyards and quaint country homes. It was so quiet, so serene, in the town this Saturday, May 6. A sense of the Divine hovered in my awareness. I wondered if something was amiss. The sanctity seemed surreal.

In fumbling the route to our destination, the quiet beauty took on enough flavor of romance for me to savor the silence. Counting my blessings, we were the only ones to arrive at the gate with no other visitors in sight after slowly winding our way up to the fortress. We wondered if this was the right castle since we were the only visitors there. After finding and reading a placard in Italian about Shakespeare's Romeo and Giulietta we were dumbfounded. "How is it we are the only ones here?" I kept asking.

At exactly noon, bells began tolling as if choreographed to our appearance. An arrival pronounced atop the castle fortress overlooking a panorama vista of lush green hills and valleys as far as the eye could see. An ethereal, divine sensation overcame me with the muted melodies echoing miles across the entire valley. There must have been seven or so varied, faint chimes ringing in melodious harmony. Serendipity Divine, I feel as if I'm stepping outside of myself, surrounded by an act of providence. The chimes of church bells is the most romantic and spiritual of sounds I love and miss.

This enchanted moment with the lightness of being, is even more pronounced after an irate exchange of wills over directions and destination. The chimes of sweet soprano tones rang with the timber of tenors in a spiritual aria carried on the breeze throughout the valley announcing the noon hour. Ascending in astonishment by foot to the top of the fortress where I stood, the phenomenon that carried me to a rare *simpatico* moment registered.

The choir of bells sent a tingle up my spine, as if my nerves were being strummed on the strings of a harp. A magic interlude with the panorama for hundreds of miles across a ringing valley, the echo of numerous church bells throughout the region in symphony, where nature and a landmark treasure will always linger as an imprint in mind from this day forward.

Newly inspired, like a gust of wind after such an experience we determined that with Ray's steadfast driving, we would make Bellagio before sunset. A mere 300 plus miles with a goat path through The Alps to maneuver the last hour. God Bless, guardian angels bless, and St. Christopher bless the fact that we made it to *Bellissimo* Bellagio without a major glitch.

When I returned home to Sausalito, several months after visiting Italy, I found Marisa of Vicenza, the Reference Librarian at The Sausalito Library. She readily shared a story about growing up near Montecchio Castle, while we stood in the library aisle selecting my reference books. "Did you know there was a secret passage between the castle and fortress?" Marisa chimes. As children we climbed through the passageway tunnel between the Montecchio Castle and Fortress on two adjacent hills. We'd get stuck in potholes, and it was very scary in the dark, sneaking our way through." That is dangerous beyond a child's comprehension, I thought. She was a brave child. Marisa thought it doubtful if this tunnel is open or even exists today since the castle serves private concerts now. I recall seeing what looked like the beginning of setting up for such a concert when we departed Montecchio that day.

Marissa also shared, "I taught grade school in the Mountains of Abruzzo, (another coincidence) where the winters were so frigid, I did not return." She was a most informative and enthusiastic librarian wanting to share and hear more of Italy. She found and referred several interesting books and was off sharing more childhood experiences. Marissa felt like a God send that day and a refreshing reminder of Italian hearts to have lived in the very location I just visited.

Chapter 11

Magnifico Milano

Nowhere in Italy is the pulse of business more apparent than in Milano. Expression is full tilt. Everyone is so animated, a la Milanese. I call the concierge Giovanni for directions to our hotel in the American Grand Milano Hotel after a three-hour drive from Bellagio. While driving into town through morning rush traffic, rush hour appears to be several hours long since it is 10 AM. Giovanni gives me directions for getting to the hotel I can't understand through broken English.

After directing Ray's driving and several wrong turns, we're obviously lost. I hang out the window and shouted to a handsome Italian boy in the next lane on a Vespa, "Dove' Grand Milano Hotel?" He motions which streets to turn, like a mime shouting out the landmarks over traffic noise and causing a halt to the cars behind us. We changed gears in the car, and in mind, finally on the right route after dodging traffic for two hours. The Vespa guy set us on the right path by mentioning landmarks and we arrive none the wearier.

Arriving at the entry desk, Giovanni, our concierge is anxious to get us on a tour that included the Last Supper painting by da Vinci. I was not in the frame of mind for a tour.

We are here in *Milano* tonight because on our visit two years prior, the Teatro Alla Scala was closed for renovation, which was heartbreaking, being one of my most sought-after destinations in the city.

Instead, we jump on a tram to the Santa Maria Del Grazie Chiesa, adjacent to the chapel housing the Last Supper. The giant Duomo stands as an imposing presence on the bustling *via.* Upon entering the vestibule after relaxing in the side garden courtyard with strikingly manicured hedges and a frog fountain, inside the vestibule I hear a confession in a muffled voice being offered to a priest.

This prompted my former Catholic schoolgirl self into the idea of giving my confession after years of neglect. I was absolutely driven to finish college and not become another rushed marriage and therefore believed birth control to be right for me at the time. When I met Ray twenty years later, he encouraged me back to attending Sunday. Since then, I have done my best to reform as a practicing Catholic.

A desire to redeem myself in Santa Maria del Grazie, while confessions were being heard, is spontaneous. Many years have passed since kneeling in the dreaded confessional cubicle. "Father forgive me, for it has been how long since my last confession?" I thought that if the priest doesn't understand English, it would be a breeze and I'd be that much more relieved of guilt. After examining my conscience, and every corner, side altar, and fresco in the church, I was still waiting for the priest to finish with the woman ahead of me. Now twenty minutes later, I see her shadow with head bobbing and distinguish her voice enough for an occasional Italian word. A heated conversation with the priest persisted.

I came up with several Ten Commandment categories that could represent the conglomerate of sins for years past after doing a best recall examination of my conscience. Awaiting my turn in the dimly lit vestibule, the woman in the open confessional continues to rattle away with despair. I wonder if this is really the right thing for me to do by now since my adrenaline reserve and childhood fears of guilt are fully engaged in gnawing at my stomach fifteen minutes later.

Appearing like a vision out of nowhere, a Bishop strides in with his white silk cap, hair, and garment. The only problem for me is, he's out in the open house of the church nave with folding chairs and without kneelers. I approach the dignified Bishop as he sat with a gaze looking out over the church and demurely ask, "Will you hear my confession in English?" He shook his head firmly and said," No, no *capisco*." I dismissed it as a saving grace rather than a disgrace. I walk away just as full of sins as the moment I entered. However, I feel closer to God and hear angels faintly singing. I knew God was listening and forgave even without a priest's assistance and thought back home I will summon the courage.

I believe that if you are a good individual with family care and give back to the community, you are well on your way to being a good Christian. The supreme commandments of "Do unto others as you would have them do unto you" and "Love God with your whole heart, mind and soul" cover it all. Church attendance alone is only rehearsal for how you live your life. Confession is a sacrament, a sacred therapy to assuage the guilt and make for living a better life as a Catholic.

Milano, Fashion First

Milano, the fashion capital is a must-see stop to shop and ogle the garment trends. Milano provides a visual smorgasbord of looking fabulous, Bella Figura, the art of beautiful people watching, in the world of high fashion. Appearance is everything…as important as the food you eat.

Back at our hotel, the room is near sauna heat with broken air conditioner. A call to the maintenance man, Fredo, whose animated gestures with his bright eyed *scusi,* excuse me for the disturbance is humorous. He keeps repeating *scusi* and sorry. Fredo is like an Italian *boffo* TV variety show caricature. I'm so exhausted with jet lag, I can't drag myself out of bed after settling in for an afternoon nap. He is timid and conscientious.

Fredo must pull the brass metal tiles out of the ceiling to get at the air conditioner. The tiles come tumbling down to the floor and he offers at least three more *scusis.*

Here at an American chain hotel, service and atmosphere is anything but American. Bravo. In a refreshing way we languish with the familiarity of a comfortable hotel from a previous stay two years prior. Gilded deluxe antiques adorned the room with fabrics of fine Italian design.

Currently, there are congressional elections being held and many, many business suits in the hotel ballroom and lobby. We witnessed lines of voters on election day for now dethroned President Silvio Berlusconi. At that time the new president Giorgio Napolitano was sworn in. Berlusconi was in office for seven years. Who would have guessed Berlusconi makes a comeback and Italian citizens vote him in over Napolitano. At that time, we find out there are at least 26 political parties in Italy. The election is held by the House of Parliament and three representatives for each of twenty regions.

The following day we window shop our way down Via Cuneo and Corso Magenta.

After all, Milano is the capital of design for countless trades. Shopping along Corso La Magenta we came to a dance shop with a chorus line of mannequins posed in high grande battement ala seconde (side leg kick), arms in fourth position, *port de bras.* Ray snaps a photo of me striking a ballet pose, mimicking the mannequins in the window display. The detailed form of these dancing sculptured mannequins is awesome to a dancer.

Then we jump onboard a tram to Teatro Alla Scala. Milano offers free public transport on the streetcars. What a treat! We kept glancing at the driver to see what we needed to pay, and he did not respond. Dove La Scala? Quickly interrupting, an auburn-haired woman seated in front of us began to argue with the nun next to her, as to the best walking route.

Off the tram, with dogged determination this woman kept on a verbal tirade, daring to contradict directions, even those of the kind nun, a woman of God's order. So, we are astonished at the direction this request for assistance takes, turning into an argument in loud, speedy, indistinguishable Italian. When we arrive at our trolley stop, we jump off and the good Samaritan woman gently leads us across the street and down a couple of blocks to Vittorio Emanuele shopping arcade to prove her argument's point. She then proceeds with animated directions to the Duomo Cathedral and Teatro Alla Scala.

A tall statue of Da Vinci stands across the way as if guarding the portals of this sacred structure for performing artists, Teatro Alla Scala. Scala means scale, ladder, or staircase. All can apply as musical scale, musical ladder or in this case staircase of the theater. I liken it to the musical scales singers and musicians climb to warm up their voices and instruments. Finally, the masterpiece finale for my last stop in Italy, a much-anticipated visit to La Scala since the renovation. The exterior of the Opera House is rather plain, nothing sensational, however, the interior is a *magnifico* masterpiece.

Leonardo Da Vinci in Piazza across the via from Teatro Alla Scala

When I arrive at the ticket concession I get word from Marcus the clerk, "They are changing light bulbs, so the theater is closed for the time being. You can still tour the museum". Not to be deterred and have my dreams drop from under me, I mention having come all this way from San Francisco, a second time to see the inside of the Opera House. Can you please at least let me see the theater seating since I have come all this way from San Francisco Ballet as a staff ballet instructor?" I meekly ask.

Marcus nods and pleasantly smiles. He hands us tickets with beautiful artwork and advises in a quiet undertone, "*Ritorno e dieci*, ten *minuti*." Praise be to the Lord. We return after an espresso at La Scala Café. On entering we are blessed to watch the set builders on stage for the ballet La Bayadere, opening in two days, Saturday night. I checked months in advance if we could see this ballet, however it was not meant to be since we were unable to get a flight that would coincide.

Opera is passion personified, it is the original venue for scandal, drama, and the start of the pedestrian television soap opera. Operettas have also sprung from this form of theater as well as English and American Broadway. Even if you're not an opera fan the art and design within are a must see.

If you have any appreciation for classical music, you will be enchanted. Nearly every major composer is represented in the museum and particularly the feeling of being in their hallowed halls of performance with the greatest musicians of their time. The scale of musical genius on these premises of La Scala is overpowering in layers of musical history with my sixth sense for the presence of past composers within these walls. It's an experience to be overwhelmed.

In the main foyer, two young men work climbing a ladder to replace the light bulbs. Their look of great pride as I stare at their movements around the chandelier needs little explanation while maneuvering around the masterpieces in crystal. About twenty giant chandeliers glisten and wrap around the parlors, bar and lobby that pour into the theater. With today's changing of the lightbulbs, we admire the exquisite chandeliers in the foyer. The theater is none other than breathtaking. The enormity of crystal chandeliers is stunning and illuminating. In the main lobby alone hang at least six enormous chandeliers the size of palm treetops. Today is the day accentuating the sparkle of these massive artworks of glass.

We chasse' up to the marble top drinking bar, not ballet barre. The intricately detailed dark wood and mirrored backdrop conjures up patrons in conversation and buzzing around at intermission. I ponder what a spectacle with the world's foremost fashion capital combined in the world's most famous opera house dancing around La Scala and schmoozing in first grade fashion with their Italian Haute courtier of Armani, Versace, Gucci, and Prada.

It's a blessing to be here outside the time of performance since we wouldn't be able to see near the detail of design and architecture with the crowds. I reflect as we have attended many ballets at the San Francisco Opera House. In San Francisco, the colorful cast of patrons in their finest fashion as the parade of fashion is nearly as entertaining as the ballet or opera itself. Attending ballet with the ceremony is my most beloved occasion. Opening-night ceremonies are graced with gourmet restaurants and chocolatiers providing canapés and champagne in the lobby.

While at La Scala, touring the scenery is a short half hour. It is more magical to see the backstage process in progress than an actual performance as lumber and artistry turns into scenery and sets. I touch the walls and stairwell railings to feel the presence of musical composers and hear their music. Original Opera Billings of the 1800s on parchment *scritto* in jet black ink hung on the walls of the halls with Verdi, Puccini, and Vivaldi. The musical geniuses that graced this extraordinary Teatro had my head spinning so, I don't recall feeling this captivated by a living, working monument to history. Civic buildings or monuments centuries old, are the only other buildings that I can think of that continue to provide the function for which they were built.

Composers worked here in the 1800s, the most prolific time of the great composers. Teatro Alla Scala is one of the original theatres known for hosting Opera Master's genius music throughout history. I am astounded, that since 1778 over 200 years, performances and productions still go on stage today in this giant theater. Rossini, Paganini, Donizetti, and Bellini.

Opera singers and luminaries such as Caruso and Pavarotti graced the stage. I am most humbled by the parade of composer's legacies throughout time here in the same monumental theater.

Verdi was the most celebrated composer in La Scala and not until the 20th Century were composers outside of Italy invited to perform their works. Mozart had many of his operas performed here. Giuseppe Verdi composer of Traviata, Otello, Rigoletto, Falstaff, and the anthem of the Risorgimento from The Opera Nabucco. Risorgimento is the tribute to the unification of Italy from the mid-1700s to 1870 and is sung today as their National Anthem.

Within La Scala's Museum, displays of musical instruments, paintings, busts, costumes, sets and numerous artifacts of the composers and performers in both ballet and opera adorn and reside in the rooms. Jewelry and coins lay beneath a glass case that pay homage to the composers. Captions are written beneath paintings and busts. Opera Announcements on parchment in jet black billing style, date as far back as the original performances of The Masters of Music in the 1800s. Portraits and billboards of Verdi, Puccini, Rosetti, Donizetti, Puccini and Mozart line the halls and stairwells. A two-hour visit was inadequate to absorb the enormity of the creative geniuses that performed here and whose spirits still linger.

Our hotel is a few blocks from Verdi's Home of Retirement. Across the street stands a large bronze sculpture of him in the median of a roundabout on Piazza Buonarroti. One evening we strolled the branch streets through a row of restaurants on either side. Across from Verdi's statue, I notice an inscription on the building's top. It reads *Casa di Riposa di Musicisti*. This home must have been a studio for musicians around Verdi's time. I later found out that Verdi funded a musician's retirement home until his royalties ran out. The sounds of glorious melodies playing from these windows and held within the walls of *Casa di Musicisti* from centuries past, bring a sense of wonder. Verdi himself lived in the Grand Hotel Via Manzoni, until his death.

Shop Till You Drop

Ray and I set out shopping along our favorite street en route to all the major monuments of Milan. The window displays are inviting and inventive at the historical Vittorio Emmanuelle Galleria and Emporium. I'm convinced the Galleria is exquisitely the grandest arcade in all the world -- five stories high of arched and domed glass ceilings. Mosaic tiles on the ground that are so intricate it feels immoral to step on such fine artisan craft.

Ray's goal is to find a navy or black sport coat in the 100-200 Euro range. Impossible. He often sets these restrictions, which tells me he only wants the pursuit. The dollar has devalued from $1.18 to $1.32 per Euro. I am looking for a summer jacket, tops, and a smart leather purse in addition to little gifts for friends and family. It is most disheartening. After two days of looking, we decide to forget about it with the exorbitant designer cost.

The next day, now our last day in Italy, Ray suggests we go in the other direction of the Monuments on the same street as Via Cuneo, and perhaps prices would be more reasonable. Sure enough, we saunter just two blocks west from our hotel on Via Washington into a department store that has sales galore and is affordable.

Two light pastel leather jackets are chanting on the rack, take me, take me. I cannot live without these at one/fifth the price of most leather jackets. One is a cream color in blazer style with detailed silver hardware. The other jacket is a blush suede snakeskin embossed with shimmer highlights. It sounds gaudy; however, it is very chic looking and fits like snakeskin conforming to curves.

I purchase summer tank tops of columbine blue with light sequin border trim and an ivory lace trim camisole with a sparkle of opalescent sequins. Bling is so hip in Southern California; it is hard to get away from in the fashion trends. I've grown to like a bit of everyday sparkle. Why have sparkle sit in your closet only for once a year or on special occasions. Make a gloomy day a special occasion!

Ray buys me a pair of Audrey Hepburn mock tortoise sunglasses in that "look at me, look" frame. My gift to him is a cool shade of purplish-blue shirt. "The color looks great on you and brings out the baby blue in your eyes," I said.

Now we're ecstatic, because I kept myself from shopping for six months back home to save and buy a few special lasting pieces here in Italy as mementos to treasure. That was no easy task, since back home we take our morning walks every day on the street of boutiques, El Paseo in Palm Desert, CA. I sometimes gaze at the window dressings for what's in fashion to wear and what I might buy.

Departure morning back home was a fiasco at the hotel. At 4 AM wakeup we were soon frantically in our Fiat to find no parking attendant in the booth outside the hotel to open the bar that blocked the garage exit to make our way to airport departure back home. We honk and shout at the booth, with no gatekeeper to be found in the booth to open the underground gate. Ray rapped again and again on the window of the attendant's cubicle without a response and ran to the receptionist leaving me sitting in the dark. I sat in the car of the cold, grey garage after a spiral ascent rounding several floors from the bowels of this gloomy underworld.

Suddenly Ricardo the receptionist hurries out with Ray and knocks hard enough to practically break the glass, merely laughing at our situation to find the gatekeeper slouched over, sleeping in the phone booth size parking booth. The guard slept through our honks, knocks and shouts. Our last bit of Italianism in Milano.

A year later, on a solo visit, Sunday morning I jump on the red line M for Metro to the Duomo. My departure from the Venetian Station is on Via Buenos Aires, a busy shopping street. On arrival at the Duomo, there was no line to get in. Amazing! I was able to hear the last ten minutes of Mass at 9AM. Because the public could not walk in the middle of a Mass, rails to block the entrance were set around the perimeter of the pews, and the choir singing reverberated to the soul like that of the Georgian chants.

Tears welled in my eyes with the purity of voices. Classical hymns move me more than any art form, sending my spirit where only joy, effortlessness, and lightness of being exist.

At the devotion station along the dark walls of the Cathedral I deposited a coin and grabbed a candle to light another candle as an offering and prayer asking God for healing thoughts. My prayers were for Ray and I to be at peace and my family to remain in good health and prosperity. My mantra became "Being worthy of all my dreams." God Bless the decision makers of this world to bring the best solutions to the table.

I then dipped my hand in the holy water font on exiting and danced my way through the Vittoria Emmanuelle Galleria past a high pedestal standing sculpture of DaVinci and onto the Teatro Alla Scala Museum.

Glory Be to God, a museum in Italy opens at 9 AM on Sunday. This was one of the best discoveries of my journey since there are only 3 other visitors in the entire museum. I follow the couple ahead of me with their private tour guide and eavesdrop on some history of the composers whose larger-than-life-size bronze busts encircle the chandeliered foyer. My mission is to find out as much about Cecchetti, one of the world's foremost ballet dancers and Masters of the 19th and 20th Centuries. His method was my foundation for ballet. Cecchetti was considered the greatest male dancer of his time and provided the most prolific technique as a teacher, born out of La Scala Ballet.

Cecchetti began performing at age 20 until the Maryanski Theater in St. Petersburg insisted upon his residency as Premier Danseur performing for many years. He retired to Italy and upon Arturo Toscanini's request and his dream to be at La Scala, continued teaching until his death.

Since age four and as a schoolgirl, I grew up with Cecchetti Ballet technique in Denver, Colorado knowing nothing else about dance until age 18. Ballet was ballet was ballet, so after studying Master techniques from around the globe at the Royal Academy of London and Vaganova out of Russia throughout my adult life, I have returned to discover Cecchetti's roots and mine here at La Scala in Milan, Italy.

The Museum maintains very little on ballet, however, the walls emanate the sounds of Cecchetti and dancers, Verdi, Puccini, Rossini, Paganini, and Vivaldi. What remains of their performed compositions is displayed on the stairwell walls in giant black and white playbills of the day. Upstairs is the most magnificent collection of paintings, sculptures, musical instruments, costumes, artifacts in coins, porcelain boxes, figurines, and fans. The most astonishing collection I've seen ever assembled through the lines of theatrical history.

One floor alone is devoted to costumes divided by parlors for each performance with original playbill. Inside the theater, I stand in the box seat and touch the crimson velvet on the padded front armrest and hear them sing of musical millennia. The entire theatre is draped in elaborately ornate crimson and gold detail. An orchestra of 80 musicians is furiously warming up their instruments with the frenetic sound of nerves before a performance.

Just outside the magnificent Opera House, the world's grandest galleria of arched, beveled glass domes, over the porticos of many major design shops and cafes provide light-filled promenades to glisten with the latest fashions and accessories. The Vittorio Emmanuelle floor mosaics and the sculptured walls of five floors rising to the glass arches create a space no less breathtaking than the greatest cathedrals in the world.

Upon entering, I am greeted by the echo of chamber music as these porticos provide pleasing acoustics. Four musicians play Four Seasons by Vivaldi. Sunday morning, at 10 AM, the soft melody sounds of music from God.

No visit through the Galleria is complete without a spin on the 'twins' of Taurus the bull. Where I grew up in Colorado, they were referred to as 'Rocky Mountain Oysters'. A twirl on the testicles makes for *buona fortuna*, good fortune, and who could count the thousands of heel spinners since the twirl spot was a funnel hole, worn down a couple of inches. After carefully and gracefully taking a turn on the balls of the bull, on the balls of my feet as in pirouette poise, I hear a 'Brava' from the circle sidelines awaiting their turn, a clap, and a smile from a young man.

I rest at the espresso café of Gucci so chicly black and white modern and step through the store to see how many thousand euros it took for a purse to hold my hundred euros in cash.

Even if I had it, "Who in God's giving world can justify such excess?" I still repeat to myself with all the Catholic guilt and vows of poverty ingrained in my brain. Miss Success shouts, "Those starving children don't know I would have a purse that could feed a family of four for a year." These voices have taken on a life of their own, batting around in my head. Another meek and humble inner voice says, "But I do." Think of how awful to spend so much on something so unnecessary.

"And who on earth, but the designer climber snobs care if you have one?" my inner voice retorts. Those shallow souls are thinking, "If I have the latest one, and you don't, I'm that much more important and knowledgeable. Certainly richer." The Sisters of Charity are singing out "Give to the poor." That other voice of success and I've made it, is saying "Wouldn't it be nice to own just one? Is that too greedy, Dear God?"

Virtue and sanity win here, and I settle for the seven-euro macchiato coffee in the glamorous Gucci café, which was enough to offer entertainment, watching passersby returning from Mass, God Bless them.

Upon my return to the hotel to pack for the train to Lake Como, the hotel reception advises me to change my ticket to Cardova Stazione as it is easier to Lake Como and far less crowded. This is poor advice I begrudge and moan about later that afternoon, deposited on the banks of Como with the grey whale suitcase in tow and a two hour wait for the ferry with an additional one-hour ride across the lake. However, every sidetrack delay has its blessing.

Scenery on board the ferry navigating Lake Como

Chapter 12

Bellissimo Bellagio, Last Stop Paradiso

You may have the universe
if I may have Italy --Giuseppe Verdi

I say, "Give me Bellagio and you may have the rest of Italy." Picture yourself hovering over Lake Como in a helicopter. The lake is shaped like a long slender woman's legs taking a short leap. You are at the northern center of the boot of Italy. Bellagio is situated at the pinnacle of land between the watery legs of Lake Como where a woman's greatest virtue lies. I started visiting Bellagio during every Italian journey, years before George Clooney made it famous simply because it has every spectacle of nature and attractions that I love.

After a long trek northwest from Venice to the southern shores of Lake Garda, driving past acclaimed vineyards, we decide by the look of Garda's rustic buildings and inhabitants that nothing measures up to Lake Como from previous visits. We are too excited with anticipation of Bellagio, so we ditch any ideas of an overnight at Lake Garda and traverse to Lake Como's eastern shore where the town of Lecco resides.

After my last trip up Lake Como's right leg, her left leg from Lecco is no less perilous than the right shore. Winding down the narrow hairpin roads adjacent to the mountain, we make a pit stop in Lecco. I enter a gas station bathroom which was one of those stand or squat hole aberrations. I pray to hit the target dead center and save those beautiful new Italian leather shoes I just paid a premium plus for, at the exchange rate of $1.48 to a Euro. I do not want my own acid wash to appear on the shoes. Who designed these primitive type toilets for female anatomies? I've seen better *bagnos* in 16th Century Spa ruins. I return to the car and relax back in the passenger seat.

A woman driving a mini-Euro car, looking like half a car, stops for gas and while pumping gas, bends over while reaching into her car for something in the passenger seat. As she returns to the driver's seat, she forgets to fully shut the passenger door, and is facing my car.

As she rounds the gas pump and takes a tight turn in front of me, the passenger door swings fully open. As her car is facing mine, I see it coming like a slow-motion magnet, frozen in place and incapable of moving soon enough. This loony *Italiana* makes a broad sweep with the door wide open and whacks right into the driver's side rear fender of our rental Fiat in the exact same location as the already present fender dent on the opposite side that was gifted to us, though unseen at the rental check out. Now we have matching dents.

The woman driver, *scusi* the stereotype, gets out saying, *"Mi scusi, mi scusi, scusi senora."* Ray wanders out of the toilet. I point to the damage, and we look at each other with a "Can you believe this?" expression. With eyeballs popping, we look to the sky praying for a reality check. "How could this dent happen in the exact same location on the opposite side of the car? "I burst out loud laughing.

The apologetic Italian woman did not understand English, so the language barrier in conversational Italian made the incident impossible to resolve. Ray says "OK, let's just let it go." After all, what's another dent when we need to get the other fender taken care of before returning to Milan or they'll charge us for the one that **didn't** happen on our clock. We climb in the car laughing and baffled.

Navigating the shoreline is both nail biting agony and breathtaking ecstasy. There is no such thing as a shoulder on the road so with one blind turn after another, fearless abandon and cautious maneuvering are required. Any driver that can maneuver this road, should receive an award, a miniature Ferrari trophy reading: "I made it up Lake Como's legs." Throw in motorcycles fearlessly passing around us with a motorcyclist convention the weekend of our visit, and you have a husband who has graduated to nerves of steel, especially after eight hours of driving.

Motorcyclists zoom by Italian style on hair raising, hairpin turns and pass us at blind curves in heart stopping fashion. As the passenger in our Euro car, I held my breath a few times, closed my eyes now and again, and in about 90 *minuti* with eyes wide open, *ecco*, here Bellagio is in sight.

After miles of a continual snake road with a direct drop to the water's edge on one side and sheer rock face of the mountain on the other, our determination remained unfaltering. What seemed hours at the end of the journey and a hundred hair-raising turns on the one-lane road, we once again willingly maneuvered for a piece of heaven. At the end of the day, we giggle in a state of glee because we've neared our favorite place on earth. I envision angels appearing over Lake Como.

Arriving in Bellagio is like the first peak of sunrise glistening in radiant shades of fuchsia and crimson. In May, the lake holds winter's watershed of the *Appenine*, Italian Alps, and mountaintop snow. So pristine and crisp in appearance, the Alpine Village is the epitome of beauty, the ultimate breath of fresh air. I take several deep breaths to fill my lungs and exhale to form a mental imprint of God's last finishing touch on earth.

I'm here at the pinnacle of land to spend five days in *Paradiso* called Bellagio. The definition of paradise is *il giardano*, "a gated garden", where supreme lake, mountain and sky assemble and ascend straight to the heavens in nature's symphony. The fork of Lake Como is a heavenly corner of the world, so close to God.

Bellagio sits on the tip or promontory known as *Punto Spartivento.* The point that divides the wind is exhilarating, surrounded by the *Appenine.* Layers upon layers of mountains rise out of the deepest waters in Italy and peak in jagged form, sending a shiver of crisp air up my spine. Clouds and sunshine cast shadows upon the mountains and lake while magnificent Italianate villas somehow cling to the cliff's edge.

Gazing north, I can even see Switzerland's alpine peaks. *Primavera,* spring is in abundance. Bountiful blooms of azaleas blossom everywhere, their vibrant colors of fuchsia and purple, gracing the green-carpeted hillside along the water's edge.

I pause and peace washes over me. I feel closest to heaven here, so let the angels sing. The majesty that is Bellagio makes all other scenic wonders take their place in line. Giuseppe Verdi wrote, "*You may have the universe if I may have Italy.*" I reply, "Give me Bellagio and you may have the rest of Italy."

Feeling home at Hotel Splendide came easy the first time. I was uncertain if the feeling of a comfort zone would return upon late arrival and feeling exhausted. To top it off, this is Saturday night with no reservation and no rooms available since the internet said sold out. The divine angels over Italy continue looking out for me.

At the front desk, Lorena calmed my worries and assures me an available room, one floor higher than our last visit. With a seemingly infinite panorama of Lake Como and The *Appenine*, our view of the Arno River in Florence pales in comparison. As I reminisce on our stay two years prior and exclaim to Lorena, "I feel at home here again at The Splendide Hotel." She beams with a bright smile and wears a pride for the natural beauty of her home as if she were responsible.

"What are some of your favorite things to do?" I ask. She delights in response, "Take the ferry to the other villages along the lake with just a ten-to-fifteen-minute ride. Varenna is where George Clooney and Julia Roberts are being filmed at a Villa after being forced to flee Villa D'Este in Como with overwhelming paparazzi."

After all, Italy invented the paparazzi. I mentioned we had seen Brad *Peeet,* Pitt as the concierge pronounced it, and Catherine Zeta Jones in Rome a few days prior, filming *Oceans Twelve* in our hotel. Lorena responded, "The stars must be following you." I spent many years working at a major Hollywood film studio meeting actors, but never in such a circumstantial fashion.

The Excelsior Splendide marks 100 years of existence this year, without fanfare. Behold a skyward fresco of astonishing beauty in a gilded frame. A giant luminous angel beckons with expansive wings as if awaiting your ascent up the stairs and on into the clouds of heaven here in Splendide Paradiso.

Bellagio Shores

Where historic architectural wonder is commonplace in Italy, certain earmarks go unnoticed. The marble mosaic floors, and three Victorian sitting areas of the lobby welcome me back to another era. Each settee is draped in soft, pin-tuck velvet and each setting display a different color – scarlet red, azure blue, and forest green.

As I gaze up into the grandiose staircase, several floors to the ceiling, the rectangular stairwell with rounded corners reveals an eye-catching pattern. The ironwork rail with graceful, rounded corners along the staircase is stunning. Italians draw as much artistic attention to the ceiling detail as much as surrounding walls and centerpieces with coffered, vaulted, mosaics, and masterpiece paintings.

Thrilled by our enormous suite, wearing four picturesque windows, I absorb the beauty that is Bellagio. The size of our suite compares to the combined space of our living and dining rooms at home. I could fit our bed in the bathroom.

Right under my window, world travelers greet Bellagio while exiting the ferries loading and unloading every few *minuti.* One could gather the pulse of Bellagio here under your nose in a day, observing *bella figura,* watching beautiful people who come in all shapes, sizes, and colors.

The lakeside promenade offers ongoing entertainment as we watch passengers, shoppers, tour groups and strollers. *Il Passeggiate,* is a prominent ritual here occurring daily at twilight, as families stroll the shops and piazzas. It is fascinating to people watch in Bellagio along the lake's edge. Visitors spend idle time awaiting the ferry.

Bellagio Ferry Terminal

Following our arrival that first day, we join in the twilight stroll of *passeggiata.* Suddenly we feel a rumble over the cobblestones as a caravan of vintage Alpha Romeo *le machine*, autos, roll past us on the main boulevard through town to gather at The Grand Serbelloni Hotel for the Institution of Antique Autos Event. Ray reverts to a teenage boy and stands with jaw-dropping excitement over the array of vehicles. All makes and models of autos putter by. Passengers and drivers of all ages don their regalia and smile as Ray hand gestures his approval with waves and thumbs up.

Sunday morning the church bells toll and clamor from the *campanile,* and echo across Lake Como. As I awaken to the ferry horn, slaps of water sound against the marina. A coo-cooing bird in a nearby cypress tree chirps as if she jumped out of the clock. I peer out the window to see one of those spectacular sunrises appearing through the clouds with rays of light fanning and streaming across the sky. Transfixed by such a sky, I mutter to myself, "I do believe in a glorious God."

Ah, it's breakfast time as we step down the staircase to the Splendide's elegant dining room. The walls and ceiling are adorned with more museum-like frescoes of angels. The darling young waiters with innocent eyes are decked in starched whites, eager to assist our table and so very personable. A beautiful Italian-style breakfast spread of buttery pastries, thinly sliced salami, prosciutto, vividly colored fresh fruit, and the ever-present espresso/cappuccino on tap welcomes our day. Crisp linen napkins and tablecloths in a striking salmon color accent the large hall. I have since come to learn that Italians don't eat breakfast - just espresso and *pane,* rolls or pastry. The spreads are for *Americanos.*

Later, while strolling along the marina, we hear a Festivity Boat with a trumpeter and shot from a cannon blasting smoke in the air. We settle into a three-hour brunch on the harbor piazza of our hotel and spend Sunday resting as Lord intended.

Peering out my hotel window, at evening's call, I see a pregnant woman standing on the dock scratching her belly, as she awaits the ferry. Her husband looks at his watch and they discuss something quizzically. They both check their watches as if to say, "go or not go," and apparently decided to stay for dinner as dusk is approaching.

At sunrise, a craftsman I deem Brutus Maximus II, a large hulk of a man, bald and plain clothed, unloads and displays his hand-carved wooden gifts. This ritual is no small task. Every day he sets up and carefully collects at the end of the day, two large cafeteria-style tables loaded with his creations. His routine with his wife is visibly coordinated right under my window. They are a welcome return from a prior visit.

Brutus holds a menagerie of animals and marionettes, salad bowls and tongs, fanciful creatures, toys, etc. His table loaded with woodcarvings is an artisan craftsman's delight. I purchased a delicate wood carved bluebird the size of my thumb painted in blending hues of blue as a gift for Mom, Madeline, or St. Madeline as we deemed her, who loves delicate creatures.

The next day, a classroom of backpack-wearing third to fourth grade children file off the ferry. They gather with their teacher for a field day that looks more like a vacation. As I smile, standing in the window above with a camera at the ready, a curious boy looks up at me and grins, waving and then rushing over to tap his teacher's shoulder, pointing to me to gain her interest.

Bellagio combines the best of everything Italy has to offer. Where Italians are warmhearted, outgoing, and friendly, Lake Como residents personify these characteristics. In such an idyllic atmosphere with pristine surroundings, there is no visible poverty. Shopping is a more interactive personal experience as outgoing merchants are engaging, compared to big cities such as Rome or Milan. If you ask, shop owners take the time to share stories and background of their art and merchandise which is *fatto a mano*, handmade in Italia. Better still, their upscale boutiques are very reasonable in all price ranges. Elegant boutiques line narrow, cobblestone alleyways and climb the hillside. Shopping for all things Italian is a delightful experience.

Bellissimo Bellagio manages to gather the best of everything in Italy. I feel the quaintness and comfort of a small village with the worldliness of a cosmopolitan resort. The easy lake access to other villages takes away any feeling of isolation and gives you a perspective of life in a lakeside community, where it feels more expansive.

You can stroll on the rounded cobblestones anywhere within a mile perimeter and find most native Italian specialty items. The convenience of shops within several blocks enables visitors to savor the true flavor and the best of everything for which Italy is famous, from glass to ceramics, silk to paper, leather to lace, jewelry to high fashion. Artisans and merchants proudly display their wares with flair. Shopping here is truly and uniquely Italian. No made in China appears visible.

Along Lake Como, original silk factories still stand and spin the local raw silk into scarves and ties, often with uneven thread and variations of color. The larger silk factories can no longer run for the design houses of Milano where they selected their favorite silks up until a decade ago. Operating expenses have forced most of them out of business. This makes each piece from today's smaller factories much more interesting and original. Silk is very affordable as well, when a high fashion designer doesn't put its label on it. If you're not concerned about displaying designer tags, this is as rich looking an article of clothing as I've seen anywhere, and stunning for a shawl or wrap.

There are dozens of villages that dot the shoreline up and down the legs of Lake Como, each one a treasure. I dream of an entire summer well spent on the lake, ferry hopping village to village, each offering its own unique flavor: Varenna, Menaggio, and Tremezzo, where one of many significant and exquisite villas like Villa Carlotta and Villa Melzi, a favorite of villas, grace the shores. The 18th Century Villa Carlotta was a wedding gift to Carlotta at age 23, from her mother, Marianne, Princess of Prussia.

Impeccably restored to its original décor by the Italian State, each room of Villa Carlotta three floors tastefully displays museum-quality art and furnishings. Paintings, marble sculptures, and period pieces are appointed in every room, too many to mention. The open-air wrought iron design elevator is particularly noticeable, and the ride is a bit unnerving. Balconies bestow a bird's eye view of fountains and gardens groomed with borders of Camelia hedges as a formal Italian garden. As I continue to gaze across the lake from the terrace, I can even see Bellagio rooftops in the distance.

Villa Carlotta is most famous for the acres of botanical gardens that surround it. Rhododendrons line up in orchard style. Many different species of Azaleas in bold My favorite are the bold fuchsia that covering the hillside down to the lake. brighten and splash the hills with color. A pergola corridor of whispering wisteria with lavender blooms cascading everywhere. stretches the length of a football field at the ferry stop near the entry to Villa Carlotta.

A vast array of vegetation from around the globe covers the hillsides. Their abundance is due to the special sediment deposited by glaciers. A fern garden of many tree species in multiple shades of green, carpets and climbs up the shadowy hillside. A narrow creek winds and runs below a crevice and meandering path. Tropical plants and citrus fruits thrive. A Japanese tea garden of bamboo, bridges, and bonsai spreads like a blanket. Coy fish swim in little pocket ponds, dotting the garden. The fresh scents invite a deep meditative breath.

Ray and I stand on a bench perched under the wisteria-draped pergola tunnel to pose for one of our favorite photos in all of Italy. A wisteria tree near the villa stands at least thirty feet high. As a slight crisp breeze wafts across the lake, delicate petals quiver and a bouquet of fragrance lingers through the grounds.

Upon return to Bellagio two years later, we revisit an exquisite romantic setting. Imagine a twilight dinner at an outdoor cafe set on the harbor's edge. A *pergola* stretches above table settings, overflowing with the lavender wisteria that defines delicate spring. The only thing between our table and the water's edge is a barrier of boulders.

Pink tablecloths are highlighted by the same shades in the clouds, while the sun sets in the dusky sky. Our waiter dodges traffic with the finesse of a dancer as he runs from the kitchen of the Hotel Florence across the road to our table. No less than a Cirque de Soleil balancing act, he carries platters of pasta and arrives at our table to announce the menu presentation.

This evening, a duck lands on the pergola and roosts just above our heads. She quacks in a painful blare as if she's lost her mate. At dinner's end, we hear rustling in the wisteria branches. Just as magical as Lake Como's twilight, comes the arrival and reunion of our duck's mate, a metaphor in celebrating our romantic evening. The sun is nearly set behind the alpine mountain peaks, so close I feel I could reach across the lake and touch the mountaintops at this twilight hour.

Some of the Northern Italian cuisines in Bellagio is infused with Swiss and French sauces over buttery pasta for mouthwatering flavor. Another hungry night we venture out to Far Out Ristorante, a strange name from sixties slang, rather odd for this part of the world. American jazz club music sets the tone for this minimal, totally chic modern *ristorante*. Sleek-looking grey and burgundy walls framing edgy modern art have me wondering if I'm cool enough to dine here since I'm not on the "A" list of rich and famous. At one table sits a dead ringer for Al Pacino. The young attendants are flamboyant young men, easy on the eyes. So sublime is the seafood fare that an encore visit is irresistible.

On return a few days later, I order the exact same meal. Why mess with success, when the encore meal is all clammed up, *spaghetti vongole.* The local red wine, *Bravissimo!* is only $5 a carafe and better than designer labels in the United States. Less than a bottle of Pellegrino sparkling water, *acqua con gas.*

Cell phone use had become so prolific by that time in Italy, the early 2000s, that one waiter while serving, was so entangled in a personal conversation, we found him outside the back door as we left. His heated discussion, as if a life and death matter, marched on even in the face of spattering rain. His motion and drama, weighed heavily, on whether the topic of discussion was significant or not. Given the Italian temperament, one rarely knows whether the sharp emotions are over a trivially broken date or a devastating death in the family.

This reminds me of other unrestrained cell phone users whom I observed across Italy. A gondolier in Venice handily juggled rowing down a narrow canal while speaking on his cell phone. The contrast of a cell phone on an 1800s gondola, goes unnoticed by the Italians. The bikini clad *signorina*, while wading in the ocean waves at Rimini, feels no need to end her cell phone conversation.

How about at the *terme*', spa in Rapolano Terme, where separation from the cell phone is not even considered by a bather relaxing in the mineral pool. Italianisms abound with cell phone situations, exemplifying their need to always connect with others.

On our last evening, everything appears translucent at twilight and a sense of the Divine permeates the air. The violet azaleas blend with the sunset hues. The sun's reflection on the lake, beams with a golden halo. A sprinkle of raindrops scatters as residue of an ending rain shower. We strolled from Hotel Splendide, down the seaside boulevard and up the terrace steps to a park named Materi de Liberte.

A precious petite old woman, my guardian angel sent from above, stands in the small terraced public park next to the main promenade. She feeds the birds breadcrumbs from a large plastic sack near the entry of a small chapel. Looking like a frail bird herself, Bella stands under a giant cypress umbrella tree, draped in the black attire of a widow, shaking her fist at the cats, shouting *gato*, for fear the cats will harm one of her brood of birds.

Traditional Italian women often take this role of widow for the rest of their lives, always wearing black, never to marry again. She is disheveled and her black cardigan is buttoned unevenly, whether this is because she cannot see or is not concerned is the question of the day. Bella is about my mother, Madeline's age, 72. My mind drifts to memories of Mom, lover of birds and gardens, and birdhouses she set up outside around our home.

Bella approaches us and we introduce ourselves. "Bella B" she replies, with a glimmer in her tired eyes and a keen awareness uncharacteristic of the age she wears. I ask her to repeat it numerous times, unable to understand this unfamiliar name through her thick Italian. Bella walks over to a small stone monument in the park and passionately tries to explain herself.

I understood about every fifth word she spoke. I began to decipher when she pointed emphatically at the stone monument, and we walked closer to read the inscription: La Libre Fascista - Giacomo Giordano September 7, 1944. "Fascista", she keeps repeating. She explains her adoration of Americans for helping save her home and paradise in Bellagio during World War II.

I cover my heart with my hand and extend my hands to clasp her face. We lock eyes on a gaze and tears well up in both of our eyes from feeling the weight of the moment and our connection in spirit.

Bella insists we follow her and proceeds to wobble down some bumpy cobblestone steps. I am astonished she could manage the stairs. Her ankles were stuffed and bulging over her worn black shoes. Bella led us to a little piazza across from the library. She points and waves her finger again at a marker stone in the surrounding wall, saying *mio marito,* my husband.

The bright white Carrara marble inlaid piece on the grey brick wall of Via Bellosia reads: Augusto Bifolco: Sindaco di Bellagio: March 7, 1895 - February 6, 1991, living long for their freedom till age 95.

I am astounded to realize her husband was Mayor of Bellagio after World War II. I later found in correspondence with her family, Augusto was the very first Mayor of Bellagio, and quite the ladies' man, not marrying until age 60. Bella was just 24 years old as a bride in 1955, such a long time to be a widow.

She then led us down a lane behind her gate and to a small garden in front of an unassuming apartment building on Via Bellosia. A gorgeous view above Lake Como greets her every day. Bella is a guardian angel for St. Francis of Assisi, the divine protector of all of God's creatures and His landscape. Her pride is glowing as she shares her garden display. Dressed in simple clothing, she makes her way up and down the bumpy cobblestone alleyway steps daily to feed the birds. Bella B is a Godsend, the angel's final touch to my Divine journey. This is the stuff serendipity is made of - a perfect ending at twilight for a last night in Bellagio. I want to spend more time getting to know Bella.

Gondola monument on the edge of Lake Como

From the heights of the Italian Alps to the depths of Italy's deepest lake, gorgeous gardens carpet the lakeshores alongside the predominant Villas of Milanese monarchs. Bellagio's resident local charm is a genuine, refreshing welcome, and calls upon my return again and again with a yearning to stay longer each time.

As a child raised at the foot of The Rocky Mountains, this region of astounding mountaintops and lakes nearly eight thousand miles away, gives me a comforting reminder of growing up in Colorado.

I sit like the duck precariously perched overhead in the pergola draped in wisteria vines at the lake's edge, singing out for its mate to discover the next best landing at the edge of paradise. Is there such a place? I'd rather freeze this moment in time when I realize it doesn't get any better than this. Here I can transcend my everyday life, knowing I can return and still feel at home. If I had a stopping place to choose, it would be Bellagio, *Mio Paradiso* in my world of Italy.

Chapter 13

The Italian Way, On Being Italiano

What is this instinct like hunger, a burning desire to discover all things Italian, searching to uncover my identity from *nana e nano's* native land? The more I discover the more drive for seeking the Italian way. I derive inspiration, craving a deeper connection to their culture of *Bella,* beautiful people in a Bella country. What do Italians do?

The hunt for the agony and bliss of being Italian tastes that much sweeter as I gain an understanding of the creative instincts that course through my veins.

The Beatitudes

Blessed are the poor in spirit, for theirs is the kingdom of heaven.

Blessed are those who mourn, for they will be comforted.

Blessed are the meek, for they will inherit the earth.

Blessed are those who hunger and thirst for righteousness, for they will be satisfied.

Blessed are the merciful, for they will be shown mercy.

Blessed are the pure in heart, for they will see God.

Blessed are the peacemakers, for they will be called sons of God.

Blessed are those who are persecuted because of righteousness, for theirs is the

kingdom of heaven.
Blessed are you when people insult you, persecute you and falsely say all kinds of evil against you because of me. Rejoice and be glad, because great is your reward in heaven.

Rooted in the life of God, as their only lasting peace, places the heart at the core of their being and character. Identifying with the heart, soul, and spirit of what makes Italians seemingly happier and less stressed, even in their frenzied outbursts, has been my quest.

"Blessed are the poor in spirit, for theirs is the kingdom of heaven" is the first of eight beatitudes of Christ, created as a model for cultivating our own virtue and character -- our heart. Roman Catholicism establishes a profound basis of Italian identity and continues to flourish throughout Italy. As Saint Pope John Paul II, (JPII) the most beloved Pope of modern times stated, "Beatitudes are a road sign to show our life's journey." Such faith and trust in Christ nurture's identity for a deeply personal and ever-lasting security beyond worldly means. The beatitudes are stamped in our hearts and souls, cultivating character and virtue.

Italian character shines from friends in Bellagio like Gabriel A. and Bella B. where they opened their homes and gave me personal tours, numerous times as an occasional visitor. The enthusiasm and sincerity with which they share their history and background to help me understand their lives, made everything about each stay marvelous. Gabriel allowed me to follow her tour guide work with a private vintage boat ride across Lake Como and opened her heart in ways friends back home have not. On another visit, she gave me a delicate glass-blown angel as a reminder of the beautiful artisan crafts of Bellagio and her angelic way.

Bella, another happenstance friend, described the history of WWII in which her mayor husband was instrumental as described in the Bellagio chapter. It is only the time in Italy, not other countries that they evoke such warmth in me.

What is it about those Italians and their ambivalent manner, masterful and misunderstood behavior, fascinating, and ingenious history? "Italianisms," a term I deemed to describe the pervasive ambiguity in their society. The fact that the Romans mastered conquest over many civilizations and developed a society that in the end, created an overbearing, gluttonous empire that altogether self-destructed is a paradox, an Italianism.

Over 80% of Italians still consider themselves practicing Catholics. In the 1970s both divorce and abortion were legalized in Italy. Even in the face of this evolution in defiance of Vatican Dogma, the family is honored above all else and divorce remains one of the lowest in Europe.

There is no rush to multi-task, and place pressure on deadlines. Think of their counterculture, "slow food" term, businesses shutting down for *pranza*, lunch, and even time for daily *sonnellino mezzogiorno*, afternoon naps. Men sneak off to play cards on their game tables or simply sit in the piazza or park benches for hours watching their world go by.

Italian's love affair with theatrics and drama has its roots in Opera. They are attracted to aesthetics and beauty. At times you do not know if the behavior and character is a performance of first-rate acting in an eccentric manner or real life. Is it real or contrived?

Luigi Branzini author of *The Italians* writes of the ambivalence of his own people. Some believe the talent of illusion is to be applauded and if the performance is believable and no harm is done, they are to be commended. One must learn to distinguish what "is", rather than what appears to be. They are natural actors donning the masks of Tragedy and Comedy.

This very type of Commedia dell'Arte and ambiguity amounts to Italianism. Whatever change of mind, fits your mood, gets your goat, turns you on, and sets you free--liken this contradiction to one who has the prerogative to change their mind. This is the way decisions are sometimes made in Italy, even of the highest order and consequence. Shrug your shoulders and live in the moment for the redeemable qualities are significant and far outweigh these human flaws of emotion and theatrics.

Commedia dell'Arte has its roots in 16th Century history here. A fine contemporary example in the film is Marcello Mastroianni, *Divorce Italian Style* from early 60s, still funny and dated in the double standards for men and women.

Another example in early history is *la pulcinella* a clown that originated in the 17th Century, used by puppeteers, and is still very much alive in the arts, a mime using a language of gesture.

Italian gestures are a language unto themselves where one motion tells a story. The flick of the fingers to the chin is often used for strong expression and brevity, like buzz off, thus the use of hands and arms flailing while speaking is commonplace for Italians even today. Perhaps their rapid cross conversations help get more in edgewise. Italians have a taste for the spectacular and embellishments are nothing extraordinary.

Every individual wants special consideration, each region its own distinction and identity. Individual identity that took until 1861 to form with the Italian Unification of twenty regions, to be named the Kingdom of Italy and known as the political movement, Risorgimento. Regional identity makes it obligatory to put on a special *festa*, festival. During the annual *festas,* the townspeople parade through the village with their patron saint statue. Festivities also celebrate harvest and seasons for fishing. There are so many saints and events honored across Italy that festivities are taking place every day.

Compare the Italian to a Hollywood actor or writer. You cannot become successful on your own without a team of logical business, left-brained thinkers. Managers, agents, publicists, etc. all support the talent of one successful artist who often thinks strictly from the right brain with creativity. Theatrics and illusion takeover and this fascination becomes their method to hide feelings of inferiority. The appearance of success is enough to satisfy and helps to transform their lives. The mindset of Hollywood personifies this.

Is it real or is it acting? Some by sheer perseverance climb to A-List celebrity status by way of scandal, intrigue, or invention. To keep creative ideas and juices flowing the artist must be able to think freely.

In Italy what began the Renaissance era are the Medici, guilds, and Popes commissioned the artists so they could free themselves of the burden of survival. They drew upon creativity rather than conquest.

In a like-minded culture, particularly socialism, it is difficult to maintain right-brain thinkers, but for the genius. In other words, a communist culture hinders creativity. The creative mind must be left to its own imagination and spontaneity. An idiosyncratic lifestyle provides the artist, inventor, or creative thinker the opportunity to be original--often an eccentric visionary.

The Italian Way

Italians are creativity personified. Ponder the thought. The right-brained thinkers of Italy, evolved after their wars when art and performance became a priority over defense and conquest. They have such a history of tragic conquest by corrupt Emperors and Papal Rule, that in Renaissance times, Italians nurtured family, while banking, papal, and ruling society competed with unmatched artistic development. It was a decisive movement in history that enthralls us today as the artistic center of the world with the key to good, simpler living.

La famiglia is still revered and cherished as the most important aspect of living Italian. In contrast to our ever-changing, ever-uprooting family values and residences in the United States and in pursuit of careers, Italy's strong religious roots based on tradition in the face of change are still striving to remain grounded. They are not without inherent problems and consequences in today's global society. Many evolving European countries wish to emulate America's dominance for business and worldly accumulation.

Sundays are still very much a custom of important gathering time for the family surrounding banquet-style meals - a day of rest as deemed by the Lord. We were fortunate to experience this tradition with our family Giuseppe and Giulia above Lake Trasemino, Umbria on the Villa Lilliana grounds.

I immediately felt a connection to their lives, absorbed in their enthusiastic welcome and warm embrace. This became the invitation to their private family and friends' Sunday dinner. The large, long farm table and benches were brought outside to the grounds between their villa and ours. Outward affection is their birthright and special quality. Their human touch keeps them in touch with life's priorities.

The linen was draped across two picnic tables and a gathering of fifteen hungry and eclectic characters assembled for the feast. The international assembly included three British, eight Italians and four Americans. The conversations that ensued were diverse and politically charged by the British contingent over American Foreign Policy.

Bella, beautiful *famiglia* is right; when you take notice of how attractive Italian families are and continue to be. I have heard there is not as much marriage outside of their country, because they want to maintain the pedigree of their traditions and culture. Understandably, and why leave Italy?

The men are often gorgeous creatures as if chiseled from Carrara marble. *Uomo*, men appear much more striking, yet not to slight the stunning beauty of many Italian women. I don't know why. Everywhere we went from the Mediterranean towns to Turin, to Venice to Lake Como to Milan there are strikingly handsome men from *carabinieri,* military police, to waiters, merchants to businessmen. Even in labor work, there are beautiful boys. If the Italian temperament and machismo are too much to live with, at least you can feast your eyes, be adored, and feel womanly. *Madre* reigns like Madonna's deity. Genders are distinct.

Just as I met very few San Franciscans who move away from the enchanting city founded by Italian fishermen, up until recent years, so too, there are few Italians with good family and community lifestyles that depart their homeland. It is difficult to imagine a better place than Italy for quality of life today.

Mainly southern Italians from the poor regions of Calabria and Puglia came to establish a better life promised in the United States during the late 1800s and early 1900s. The extraordinary benefits make anywhere else hard to compare. I left my heart in Italy, not just San Francisco.

Those born into Italy, without wealth or importance offered by their nation, have created self-importance and adventure. Wealthy family dynasties have remained prominent for over 600 years. A penchant for performance runs through their veins like thread runs through a tapestry. The sweet revenge of a poor man's life is the appearance of living richly or beyond his means. Theatrics and illusion takeover with this fascination. The appearance of success is enough to satisfy and helps to transform their lives. Is it intrigue or is it an invention?

For Italians, the ambiguity with which decisions are made and the contradictions that rule their lives seem to keep their creative juices flowing. Routine means boredom so conjuring up new ideas becomes a part of their makeup. Never mind the bureaucratic quagmire when it comes to administrative needs.

Contradiction is an Italian's good friend; a way of living *la dolce vita* without stress and taking oneself too seriously in any one decision, particularly day to day. When an Italian tailor in California tells me, "The hem in your slacks will be sewn and complete next Tuesday as you wish, do not worry." He may not intend to have it complete, however the tailor views that temporarily pleasing you at least until next Tuesday is a service itself.

The tailor feels satisfied even fibbing, by making you temporarily content, providing the expectation in your mind through Tuesday. So long to "the customer is always right" in America.

I spoke with my Dr. in San Francisco and mentioned our latest Italy trip. He shared his experience in Bellagio in the winter years ago. "All the hotels were closed for the winter but one. This one, they had *buona fortuna,* the good fortune to be inhabited by just one other guest. An American priest who was sent to dry out. The hotel had turned off the heat since they felt it a waste with just 3 guests," said Dr. Andrew. Ah yes, the quirks of Italians in the Italian Way.

Another quirk of Italians is their love for at least one good argument a day. You'd think that tempers flaring in upheaval would be a matter of life and death. It could be as little as a difference of opinion for the best directions to drive today. The beauty is how quickly forgotten and forgiven, countered with many laughs, true agony, and bliss for a daily dose of vim and vigor -- drama. Perhaps to feel their blood pulse and spark, they create conflict creating a ritual for feeling alive with the adrenalin of fight or flight. My father Vicenzio was true to his bloodline as a testimony to this. We would avoid coming home evenings sometimes, as youngsters, to escape the unpredictable fury of Dad. My ballet training and performances served me well in this regard.

The complication in most matters helps Italians feel more alive. Chaos often ruled our household of seven children. Even organized chaos took no precedent. I was brought up to believe bad things just happened without your control daily. This is somewhat grounded in leaving things to God, the Pope, and the Catholic Church. Small wonder in my adult life I became a control freak however, learning later in life starting in college, that we **can** control a better part of our destiny with planning and the choices we make. It is when you are looking for options or run out of options that we most seek God. Our country of democracy, America is founded "In God We Trust." We follow the path of our God-given gifts and talents, which makes us exceptional from others when we design our destiny with a dedication to achieving, experiencing joy and success in line with the Divine.

In Italy the art of people watching, particularly on the piazzas whether sitting or strolling, hugging, kissing, singing, playing music, or *mangia,* eating is not just a pastime. It is a way of life. *Bella Figura* means you look good, have a lovely figure, dress in fine fashion, or make a good impression. This plays into the art of people watching, not considered just some way to while away the day.

A sincere dignity exists in being a good neighbor or community living with open arms. I don't need to live for work, collecting things, status symbols or accumulating wealth. I work to live and find peace and truth, a quiet enjoyment as if to say my life is sweet and at peace, living Christian values. *La dolce vita* exists from poor to privileged because of this special inner quality of character.

The paradigm in Italy is a religious and disciplined country of Catholicism. Italians show mastery and discipline in their art and yet are spontaneous in expressing their emotions. They enjoy a bit of lack of structure and creative license in their daily lives. The paradox can be very frustrating in strict disciplinarian countries to the north, and one can only laugh when caught in their business decisions based on intuition and impression rather than business principle or fact. Children stay at home with parents longer not only for financial reasons, also because of the family continuity and less conflict between generations.

La passeggiate is their evening-time custom to gather with friends and casually stroll on the streets where you live, a tradition amongst residents in their communities as a daily event to talk and commune. The young mix with the old and reinforce the generational bonds within the community. They window-shop and discuss significant and insignificant issues with friends, neighbors, even strangers. The evening stroll reveals the spirit and beauty of a community.

Italian's wonderful sense of expression and community shines an example to others lacking throughout our nation today.

One of the reasons we are so stressed with no time for relaxing, winding down with family, friends and acquaintances or talking nonsense and unsolvable world issues is that digital communication has overtaken the humanity of socializing. Media platforms are controlling not only our business lives but our personal identity as well. Italians often seek out connections and relationships daily with others, particularly displayed in every town piazza with the old men watching and commenting on the world going by their benches.

The national flower of Italy is the lily. That brings my favorite flower, the Stargazer Lily into a special light - meaningful like the creative genius of astronomer Galileo, gazing at the stars.

Creative imagination for children in America is going extinct due to television, computers, and digital devices. Without the time encouraged to use their imagination and social interactions, children become nonsocial, moneymaking machines in our culture.

I hope as a culture, we can reawaken the need for handwork and creative genius stimulated through moments of quiet imagination. Perhaps then our values will change away from overconsumption. I believe observing and integrating Italian life today with *il dolce far niente,* the sweetness of doing nothing combined with traditions will help restore harmony and value in our everyday lives. I pray that American society does not repeat the history of the Roman Empire that demolished itself due to greed and gluttony, not only of the powerful leaders but all citizens with an ambitious lifestyle in our country today.

The Tarantella folk dance often illustrates an Italian state of being. The allegro dance is performed in circles at Italian weddings, gaining speed and quickly changing direction and continuing to speed up again for those who can keep up. Tarantella is derived from the tarantula spider and is likened to the sporadic movements when bitten. The Italian zest for life is portrayed in this dance as I see lived out in our frenzied lives today.

Chapter 14

Fatto a Mano, Made In Italy

My husband Ray suggests after traipsing through many shops, that a benefit of being my friend is the urge to bring back a piece of Italy from whatever is famous in the town or region we visit. I find a portable version to present to friends.

Ray voices his complaint as I diligently walk from shop to shop finding that special little memento for friend or family member. He says, "You're the only person I know to go to such great lengths while on your own vacation." The joy of the search and discovery in what I learn of the people, their region, traditions, arts and crafts, makes it rewarding for me. The *sorriso,* smile of joy that registers on my friend's face makes it all worthwhile

Centuries-old artisan crafts such as silk ties and scarves from Lake Como have been manufactured for hundreds of years, originating in the 1400s by Duke Ludovico Sforza of Milan who planted mulberry trees around Lake Como where silkworms spin their threads. A handcrafted silver necklace, from silversmith Bulgari designed since the 1880s makes distinctly one-of-a-kind jewelry, a trade handed down for centuries gleams in the display window. Or the hand-blown glass ornament from a factory outside of Venice unique in the Veneto region is testament to the pride and possession of such artisan trades for centuries.

Murano glass of Venice mini in shades of blue with a pendant of millefiori and two doves in flight

That little treasure becomes something very special as a memento both in memory and the joy of giving. A story I love telling and a little sample of the Italian culture. There is nothing more gratifying to the spirit than creating something by hand, something American culture has quickly lost to consumption. Specialty fields that require knowledge are eliminated because of their manual labor-intensive necessity.

The next natural step of this gift giving evolved into sharing my passion for everything Italian to the world by writing.

Wherever the town or region ventured, I seek out the artisan craftsmen for which that region of Italy is famous and proceed to find a portable version of such a *fatto a mano,* a handmade treasure to bring home as a gift or memento. Ceramics in Deruta, masks, and paintings in Venice, blown glass in Murano, hand loomed lace in Burano, wood inlay in Sorrento, painting gold leaf to refinish a frame, and lemon everything in Amalfi. Bringing Italian artisan crafts home became my delightful quest. Every merchant offers a story of the artist or craftsman distinctly their own with the gift I purchase.

Goldleaf painting restoration Master craftsman

Each little gem becomes a worthy memento because of the pride in family or community traditions handed down through centuries still handcrafted, not created for speed or cheapness, but to last with quality and the creator's inspiration. With a sample of Italian culture, in a gift carried from Italy, the joy and appreciation that registers on my niece, neighbor's or friends' happy faces, makes it all worthwhile.

It is particularly gratifying to see Italian made since I notice back in 2006 that Americans are so driven by consumption for cheap goods and labor that we outsource manufacturing all around the world. I am reminded of an internet spoof being circulated that read:

> John Smith was awakened by his alarm clock (made in Japan)
>
> And enjoyed a cup of coffee set for brewing (made in China)
>
> Listening to the radio (made in Taiwan)
>
> Shaved with his electric razor (made in Hong Kong)
>
> Put on a shirt (made in Italy), designer jeans (made in Singapore) and leather shoes (made in Italy)
>
> Cooking breakfast in his microwave (made in Japan)
>
> Set his watch (made in Switzerland)
>
> Sat down to look for a job on his computer (made in China)
>
> Got in his car (made in Germany), filled it with gas (from Saudi Arabia)
>
> And continued looking for a good-paying American job.

Sicilians carve marionettes in gladiator regalia wearing the status of ancient armor and shields. Pinocchio comes from a craftsman named Geppetto. He is true to life, Geppetto, the marionette maker of the famed Disney animation film. He has carved out Pinocchio of all sizes for decades in the rocky cliff town of Orvieto which sits atop a plateau.

A miniature stage of plywood, eight-inch square, is painted and gilded with capital columns and curtains in three dimensions. A dancing ballerina is on stage with a leg lifted in arabesque, which extends higher by way of a marionette string. Swan Lake rings out with the soothing sound only a music box provides.

In San Francisco, Flax is the name of the Artist's Supply Store and is found on Market Street in the heart of Castro. Set on a very colorful corner, this treasure trove is a must see for artists and those wanting truly unique gift and shopping experiences. I find a music box from Florence which may sound somewhat childish yet at the same time soothes the adult soul as an escape. A prized possession added to my music box collection and found in Flax the gigantic specialty store here in "the city." It would take an entire chapter to list some of their unique items. Like a room of archives, one giant room contains file after file of drawers filled with paper for paintings and collages.

Back to Italy, I'm in awe of the time and talent of artisans who handcraft everything from paper to glass, woodcarvings to silk, and leather to wine. The joy in discovering and absorbing their region, traditions, arts, and crafts, through the process makes it even more gratifying and lasting for life.

Cuisine, *Mange*

One of the most famous cafés, coffee shops, frequented by politicians and celebrities since 1903 lies in Turin with the Bull Insignia-Café Torino. It has always maintained elegant furnishings and chandeliers allowing meetings for quiet reserve. The wood carved bar is merely majestic. Café bars epitomize social gatherings and wake-up spots, coffee is a part of the Italian social diet for centuries.

The aroma of espresso is wake up in the morning. *Café*, coffee is now a social phenomenon here in the United States only in the past thirty years. Coffee houses have become the meeting bars and discotheques of the seventies, now often replacing bars/lounges serving alcohol. Italian Roast has a dark and deep flavor. Cappuccino, Latte, and Espresso all originated in Italy with milk or cream and cappuccino is strictly for breakfast by Italian standards. Macchiato is an espresso with just a topping of whipped milk or cream.

Gelato that is made from milk and egg whites instead of all cream is delicious and distinguishable beyond ice cream, as we know it. Freshly churned and whipped every day at gelateria's make it my favorite of all Italian treats if I had to choose but one. Stracciatella is a top flavor with a blend of vanilla cream and chocolate chips. The most famous gelateria we know of is right off Piazza Navona in Rome.

Italian winemaking *vino*, wine had its origins in the grapes here for centuries. Do memories of Italia go without *vino*? From Chianti to Cabernet the art of winemaking originated with the Romans. The French followed suit and added their version. The clean green of vineyard rows terraced on hillsides is pristine.

Ray and I have grown grapes and bottled wine in Sonoma and made freshly distilled limoncello. I've tried my hand at pasta but *basta*, not my specialty-Ragu and Bolognese sauce are. Balsamic vinegar is a derivative of the grape particularly famous from the town of Modena. Olive trees produce olives and olive oil, as ancient as the ground to provide a staple here.

Roma tomatoes are considered best to make *bellissima* tomato sauce and salads. *Caprese insalata* combines tomato, basil, and buffalo mozzarella cheese for a delectable fresh salad drizzled in olive oil and balsamic vinegar. An antipasto salad can have a variety of meats, with capicola, prosciutto, salami, and olive loaf. Sausage from wild boar is a highly regarded delicacy.

Lemons grow in abundance along the Mediterranean. Limoncello is a favorite aperitivo or digestive. Fresh almond candies and cookies roll around and melt in my mouth. Marzipan is the sweetest of sweet candy almond paste that melds into any shape you sculpt. The Amalfi Coast bakers mold marzipan into bright colorful shapes of fruit too beautifully sculpted to eat. Amaretto is a wonderfully sweet liqueur from almond extracts.

Biscotti – Italian hard cookies are twice baked with origins from Abruzzo, my ancestral region. No wonder I'm known as a cookie monster.

Pizzelle is another favorite cookie, particularly when Dad baked them. I remember on special occasions the aroma of anise, as a special memory of Dad making the wafer-thin waffle rounds in a waffle iron, usually flavored anise, delightfully crispy and thin. They also come in lemon or caramel flavor.

Prosecco and chocolate truffles are additional sweet *aperitivo*. Prosecco is a light bubbly Italian sparkling wine like champagne with more delicate bubbles and finer to taste.

My home is full of Italian treasures collected while traveling throughout Italy and each memory reflected when I see them makes me smile and happy.

Sorrento, Sweet Sorrento, Land of the Limoncello

Since my home is fashioned as an Italian Villa, a giant clear glass vase full of lemons adorns the table centerpiece. I made my first batch of Limoncello with lemons from our own tree, which Raimundo picked with the wire-clawed fruit picker. The only potent 190-proof, 90% alcohol I could find is Everclear, with marinating lemon peels and sugar that makes for an easy recipe and a blast off good refreshing aperitif or mixer. I purchased beautifully shaped little bottles tied with ribbon for this great summer refreshment and sipping diversion for which friends and neighbors join in.

One Saturday afternoon, Irish friend Shannon and neighbor Tess in Palm Desert, were most delighted with my gift of homemade Limoncello to make Tess's favorite Lemon Drop martini. Nothing in life appeared lemony that day. We were flying lightly, and I was very careful to slowly sip since Tess poured the little bottle of 90% alcohol into 4 martini glasses along with Citron Vodka without her knowing the alcohol content. You could say they were looped!

In the town of Sorrento, linen boutiques line the shopping paths and alleyways. Cut lace cloth with lemon appliqués. Where lemon blossoms' sweet fragrance awakens the senses to spring with anticipation of the ripening lemons. Everywhere I look appears an array of lemons. No one can escape the influence of lemons since the 1800s.

Sorrento offers a prized addition to my music box collection-a wooden inlay music box of flourishes, singing the song of Sorrento, which I purchased in a little back-alley boutique on a Sunday morning. I hear Dean Martin crooning "Sweet Sorrento."

Landscape

I love to gaze on the planted fields of poppies and sunflowers growing wild and scattered randomly across hillsides in spring. Red poppies, delicately grace and dance next to neatly planted fields of green vineyards. Sunflowers, burst with yellow brilliance, as their faces turn to greet the sun and awaken the spring. Purple Iris flag the day with elegant beauty in all shades of the other local flowers, lavender, and violets.

Then there are the cypress trees. Rows of Italian Cypress that stand like Roman Soldiers as a moniker to their land. Dark green rising like shadows on pointe toward the sky. Row upon row salutes the entryway to many villas and palazzos as if to greet the guests in a formal ceremony. The cypress scent of freshness brings a welcome entry.

Olive trees glisten greenish grey in the sun. The topside of the leaves is dark olive green and underneath the pastel grey appears silvery light. Olives are such a staple of Italian cooking you can barely escape a meal without either a *muffuletta*, an olive paste, a drizzle of oil in sauces, or a dip and soak for bread most commonly with balsamic vinegar. Over 90% of our olive oil is imported from Italy because the expense in making by pressing, etc. is far too much to be cost effective.

White truffles are the prize fare of cuisine. Rare and found by pigs or dogs, trained for unearthing truffles in Northern Italy from under the soil, white truffles are priced like gold per pound; last checked $3,000-$4,000 per pound. The flavor is permeating, distinctive and rich.

Another direct import of at least 90% from Modena, Italy is the balsamic vinegar capital of the world. Wine fermented longer becomes vinegar, as I know too well from a batch of Merlot my husband and I over fermented in the process of making our own. Evans/Evans producing a namesake wine, "For Evans' Sake" at our Sonoma, Healdsburg home.

Gardening became a form of therapy for me in the wine country where you can grow just about anything with the fertile lava soil. That's why Italians first landed in Asti, Sonoma County in the 1800s near Healdsburg to grow grapes. Fruit orchards were prevalent as well.

Until my forties, I was against anything that resembled being a domestic housewife who relished the role. I grew to love growing things starting in Healdsburg with lava soil for vineyards. Nurturing plants to grow, bloom, and harvest became my therapy. Further on, I dared to take gardening to Palm Desert after such good fortune in my lovely Healdsburg home.

Planting in abundance became my leisure pursuit in Healdsburg. Our slogan became, *Do as The Romans Do*, which is plant and grow grapes. Cultivate your own backyard vineyard. And so, it is. We terraced the soil, planted, harvested, fermented, crushed, bottled, and packaged our own Merlot vineyard. Almost all our wine bottles were gifts for friends and family of nearly twenty cases of wine produced. Dozens of roses and gladiolas lined the backyard perimeter with iris, hydrangea, butterfly bush, wisteria, jasmine, columbine, lilies, and various annuals spilling out of wine barrels overflowing flowers.

I nurtured a vegetable garden of tomatoes, bell peppers, squash, and lettuce, herbs of lavender, mint, basil, and oregano in abundance. And to think giving it all up wasn't that hard for me because gardening was taking over my life. Me, the one who loves to travel to Italy -- this put a cramp in my up-and-go living. I'd worry about watering and care while away.

In Healdsburg, Tony was the self-appointed caretaker of the Bocce Ball Court where every morning he groomed, raked, and practiced his Bocce. The court sat on the west side of Healdsburg High School Stadium with old aluminum bleachers. On the north side is the most incredible handcrafted hardwood playground maze I've ever seen. The play tower was constructed by the local fire department and community volunteers. It stood two stories high and had all the frills of slides, monkey bars, bridges, etc. for a primo playground.

After five years of visits, we were entranced by Palm Desert enough to make it a home, il *Italiano* along with our Sausalito land yacht. My Italian designed landscape in the desert is filled with bougainvillea, roses, and iris of Italian/Mediterranean gardens that miraculously withstand summer temperatures up to 115 by proper shade placement and watering. I brought several hibiscuses from soggy Sausalito that survived for years in the desert with a touch from above. Even a gardenia tree planted in the shade with TLC blossomed heartily.

I love growing basil for meals. Basil in Italy is the sign of love. It is used as an herb, a garnish, a sauce, a paste, a *pesto*, a salad vegetable, etc. It is the easiest herb to grow next to oregano. Basil mildly spices many tomato sauces. Caprese salad made of fresh basil, tomato and buffalo mozzarella cheese is my favorite antipasto. Pesto over linguine is my favorite primo entrée with crushed basil as the main ingredient.

We hosted a Sunday Champagne Brunch and photo show just three weeks after returning from Italy. Guests included neighbors, associates, and friends. Brunch included all Italian Fare. Antipasto with Caprese Salad and Primo bell pepper and cheese omelets and grilled Italian Sausage for our primo entrée. Ravioli with Artichoke drizzled with Garlic and Garden Oregano Oil; Asiago with Parmesan cheese sticks and ciabatta complimented the main dish. Biscotti and espresso followed a Birthday celebrated with fresh blueberries and strawberries atop a classic cheesecake. No Gelato to be found here, boo hoo.

Prosecco and Chocolate Truffles arrived as gifts in addition to several champagne bottles. I prefer Prosecco to champagne since it is a light bubbly Italian sparkling wine, smoother to swallow. A giant clear glass vase full of lemons adorn the table centerpiece. With reminders of Italy throughout our home fashioned as an Italian Villa, it all felt like Italy revisited and reminiscing. My home is full of Italian cultural treasures collected while traveling throughout Italy.

Spanish Steps Roma

One early Monday morning on our first venture to Roma as husband and wife, we lingered at a gathering place for mostly the young and chic. Here at the Spanish Steps, we indulged on our last day in Italy since I was determined to find a little local painter's painting.

I came across such an artist's painting of Piazza Navona. The seller said his brother is the painter and he hesitated to be seen with our money exchange. Perhaps he was not allowed to sell there, hence the trepidation. There on the balcony above the Spanish Steps and on the Piazza of the Spanish Embassy we exchanged Euro for this prized little postcard size find of mine. A painting of Piazza Navona, the most famed and ancient of gathering places for both Romans and tourists summoned scenarios to romanticize its origins. The beauty is enhanced by the glorious artistry in fountains and architecture that flourish in the pastel sunset colors.

This rouses a memory of a holiday trip to Paris. My long-standing quest is to find classical Degas, the master of ballerina paintings and sculpture. Upon entry to the Galerie Regis Langlois, just off Rue de Rivoli and around the corner from our St. James Hotel, I could see the artist in the backlight of the gallery, studiously painting away reproductions. What a difference between the gallery owner's and artists' personalities. The owner was merciless at negotiating the price. Jean Luc the painter was smiling when we requested his famous reproduction painting by Degas in an exquisite antique gold and baroque frame. This Degas is of one of the most recognized impressionist era ballerina paintings, spotlighted on the opera stage with dancers surrounding the wings and stage drapery.

A *Bellissimo* painting of an Italian landscape was created by an artist we located on the Piazza Navona, Roma open market—a room centerpiece to display over the sofa. An antique sepia style of Bernini's fountains and St. Agnes Duomo. What pleasures at home to have mementos of every trip reflecting the culture, cuisine, landscape, architecture, art, and friends, all the personalities of the country and regions to rejuvenate my spirit. I relish and await the joy of discovery and the next adventures in Italy.

Il Colore, The Colors of Italy

The colors, *il colore* of Italia are bold and daring. Since fine art is the God given Italian heritage, *il colore* boldly dances across buildings, frescoes, paintings, and people. Upon my initial visit to Italy in 1989, what I first viewed as unsavory, the aged colors on buildings in disrepair, I now marvel and take great pleasure. Faded, scraped, and distastefully splotchy, the irregularities or "distressed" look as we have deemed in the United States, speaks of maturity and resourcefulness sustaining through the ages.

The color originally designated on an ancient building carries the tradition and maintains authenticity, structures that resound of antiquity and whisper romance. Picture the original builder, mason, and architect -- Touch the walls to sense the significance of a structure's origin, history, and spirit.

Our home in Palm Desert is awash in Italian earthen colors -- our little Italian Mediterranean Villa. Walls of sun-kissed yellow, bold terracotta, and sea foam shades of water, are all reminders of this colorful country. An arched front entry doorway welcomes in burnt sienna. The exterior is awash in bright white stucco. The garage door is a centerpiece of cedar in the rustic style of a countryside villa with old brass rings and latches; as if to pull open the door. Both side gates match the door of cedar accent with their styled arches opening alongside and into the backyard.

Our cedar garage door was a must since a majority of the garage door covers the front and is unsightly in architectural terms. I insist our chosen home is interesting in an Italian façade.

Stone is applied to the exterior stucco by my brother, a Master craftsman and mason. He is helping create the artisan style in now our second version of an Italian home. This rough looking stone climbs from the ground and halfway up the house lining the stucco in rose tones. The kitchen window is arched in stone with a family crest or cartouche centering the arch above the window and surrounded by stone.

Ray stacked stones in a line as a border on either side of the driveway and along the curb front. Most of the stones were kindly donated by Bob our neighbor, who in his eighties often walks by our house on his strolls. Bob grew up in Napa and has interesting stories of the Mondavi vineyard for which he at one time was employed as a barrel cleaner.

An ambitious project is to pave the pool deck in a pale terracotta finish over concrete which makes it a soothing scenic surrounding and cooler to walk on. It has been a few stages of trial and controversy since the craftsman sees the finish differently than I envision it. Today I hope to get the fourth sample, which is back to my original texture and color. I have not given up, for these two workers are laboring in temperatures over a hundred in late June. Marco originally predicted two days to finish turning into two weeks -- such can be the nature of contractors. Lucky if they show, even better if on time, once a large sum deposit is made to complete our project.

Americans tend to think new is better. Replace or throw away is our daily way, rather than restoring or reconstructing. We, who have the luxury of overconsumption. Over time our tastes have cultured and matured to appreciate an aged with time and elements, distressed look. So much so, designers have reproduced it in paint finishes, furnishings, buildings, etc., ala 2006. There's an irony in reproductions, creating something new to look old. Now our contradictions play with Italy's past and present.

Another hugely popular finish is faux, as in reproduction--fake. Creating a finish with paint on walls, columns, etc. to appear like real stone such as marble, granite or travertine is a fine art. Crackling, glazing and antique finishes all in the faux line give apiece or structure instant aging. Italians have been practicing faux for ages, particularly when a budget is limited for materials.

Trompe l'oeil is another painted art form of magnificent proportion. Painted scenes on walls and ceilings often create an illusion of two and three dimensions. Many scenes throughout Italy have been imitated and made as murals on walls, to replicate the grandeur of art and scenery. Human figures, animals and nature dominate this art form.

There was a Renaissance of sorts in the United States early 2000s to duplicate distressed appearances and the beauty designed by nature's own deterioration. Particularly popular in the past few decades, distressed looks, faux finishes and trompe l'oeil are now abundant. A refined, acquired taste and surge in our country creates an era in design history for America.

Venezia, Venice changes color like changing faces in all her disguises.

The canals of Venice, all 150 of them, change hews like a shimmering two tone silk of golden aqua and murky taupe. This coloring so mesmerized me that I draped our Master Bedroom in the gorgeous transforming silk. The bedroom above all others is for soothing solace and rest to provide a calming effect and hence the room is named Venezia.

The design is to replicate both bedroom and bathroom to feel like an indulgent spa. The walls of both are splashed in a sea foam pastel tone that interchanges with light at different times of day in either shade of green or blue. Just as light shines and diffuses into varying shades throughout the day, so do these walls of color.

The play of color and light fascinates me. Resort Spas are awash in shades of this color. Green Rooms in theatres and studios are named as such, due to the calming effect of green for performers just awaiting their stage entrance. Hospitals often prescribe to green walls to calm patients.

Just off the bedroom glass sliding door, my vision of Venice appears in the shape of a pool with aqua waters and an overflowing fountain on the spa. Streaks of light dance in the water and frame iridescent pieces of mosaic shapes like the mosaic tile accents in the bathroom. The light streaks float atop the surface, then suddenly dive to the pebble stone bottom of the pool when waves splash about. Fuchsia bougainvillea blooms dance atop the waters occasionally, when blown from their climb up the whitewashed stucco walls.

Painted walls throughout my home are a buttery wash of apricot cream. The interplay of color invites a warm welcome feeling showering light around the living room, family, and dining room, kitchen, and guest room. In an open-air floor plan with three sliding glass doors and seven windows, these apricot walls wear many hues throughout the day.

The large open kitchen invites cooking in abundance with counters galore. I can dance across the floor from one cabinet to the next. Dark cherry cabinets with matching wood shutters are reminiscent of Italian window shutters. Kitchen stools at the counter make for great entertainment while hosting guests. Italian ceramic dishware from Deruta decorates the walls and counters in the form of plates, pitchers, vases, and condiment servers for oil, vinegar, sugar, and cream.

Smart looking with all the necessities for a home kitchen, I am fully into the nesting instinct when warming the oven and fires for meals. It is extremely rare in my kitchen to follow a recipe. Cooking with recipes is a chore and takes away the creative bend of a dish. Variety is the spice of life and with many herbs from my garden; no two meals are exactly alike.

Usually, I take what is in the refrigerator and make the best of a meal that I can, known as *avanzi*. A great chef for hire creates recipes and entertains the taste buds with visual patterns on a plate.

My furnishings and artwork were chosen to replicate styles of Italy all sought after at an affordable cost. The sofa and sitting chair is upholstered in gold and cinnamon red chenille. Scroll flourishes in the fabric embellish the design in a traditional style. Curves and arches are apparent in nearly every piece. Fresco-style side tables with cabriole legs were created by an Italian artist living in Montana and frame each side of the fireplace. The distressed stucco matches a mirror that hangs above the mantle. Paintings and tapestries all hang above rugs of cinnamon, terracotta, sage, and gold.

Reminders of a Mediterranean landscape loaded with blossoms of color surround us. Fuchsia and golden peach bougainvillea climb walls and arches over side gateways. The poppies of red spring up and sway on their skinny stems, while the purple iris flags their support of color and joy for the day.

The front yard is outlined with rows of pine color Italian Cypress. A palm tree stands center and the grey green leaves of the olive tree shine silver in the sun. Large yellow sunflowers line the backyard wall along with star jasmine, gladiolas, and coral climbing roses. Several delicate buttery yellow Roma roses tipped with magenta stand on their own. A single white rose bush graces the top of a mound over our beloved departed West Highland white terrier, Ziggy.

The day after Ziggy dog died, a Divine Moment descended upon us. Just above the white buds of the rosebush where Ziggy lay, an exotic white bird like a cockatiel, circles overhead. I alert Ray of the pure white bird as our eyes gaze on the ethereal vision at the same time. My senses sharpen and I become acutely aware. The cockatiel like bird lands on the top of the roof and perches on the arched edge of white stucco. The phenomenon stares out and remains still several minutes, just yards from Ziggy's resting place. The morning's light brightly displays a dawn of heavenly beauty.

A calm and serene sense of timelessness washed over both Ray and me this morning as our eyes are glued on the cockatiel-like bird with yellow tufts for hair. At that exact moment, the classic radio station began playing *Dvorak Symphony No 9, Adagio Largo aka, Coming Home*. The music resonates with a haunting symphony that stirs a vision of birds soaring high over hills and toward the sea. A surreal eerie oboe, violin strings, and horns with the grandness and solitude of Taps urge me to look to the earth's curve for sunrise.

A familiar tingle accompanies something both Divine and dreamlike. Tears began streaming from my eyes and a veil of silence and loss of our guardian angel hovers in the air.

The interplay and choreography of the music *Coming Home* with the bird in flight made us both keenly aware, without saying a word to one another, that this is a symbol of Ziggy dog, free from previous months of pain. I am now at ease in my grief knowing Ziggy is peacefully coming home; an encounter that transcends explanation, time, and life. After the graceful adagio, the bird takes flight south towards the Santa Rosa Mountains, half a mile from our home. I never saw the bird before, nor did I see it again.

Chapter 15

Italian Faith in The Divine: Miracles, Angels, and Saints

To be Italian is to be blessed. What really personifies Italians is the light of Divinity that shines in their heart, soul, and spirit. The belief that the Lord is present in their lives every day and placing their happiness in the hands of God as the ultimate source -- not in worldly things. God provides their support to overcome adversity and endure sacrifices. Their trust in Divine life after passing from this life leads to eternity and frees them from pressures others might encounter-- trust in Divine Providence with the grace of God to attain heaven.

Italians believe God is the only one truly in control, thus their less stress manner. The belief that all in the world can be seen with our mind, and all that is Divine is seen with our heart underscores Italian culture -- belief in miracles, grace, angels, and saints. Theirs is an enlightened sense of the everlasting beyond this earth -- an intuitive intelligence of faith with a deeper understanding of the invisible power of God.

You hear the bells from the *campanile* ringing, resounding off the stone walls as you pass a church. Today over 900 churches exist in Roma alone. You can discover an unexpected masterpiece painting or sculpture unannounced within the walls of a church. You may meander into a nave and down the aisles to find many side chapels, altars, or porticos with several levels of breathtaking original artwork adorning the walls by illustrious painters and sculptors such as Bernini or Raffaello. How vital a force is their belief in Christ, their faith in God, and religious ceremony as gloriously illustrated during the Renaissance. Da Vinci's envisioned attempts at flying with wings, highlight the ever-motivated Italian genius, in addition to his exhilarating artwork and hundreds of engineering prototypes.

Italians expect and anticipate miracles through prayer, pilgrimages, and devotion to the Almighty. Their radiant sense of the Divine permeates the core of their souls and sets them beyond material things into a spiritual world of grace that we often misunderstand. By aspiring for the stars and believing in miracles and eternity, their lives are enriched through faith and joy in simpler worldly pleasures and family traditions.

Apostle Matthew wrote in verse 22:37, the great commandments from Jesus, "You shall love God with all your heart, mind, body, and soul. Italians live to "Love thy neighbor as thyself." As a daily witness, to their extensions of kindness and grace countless times, I'm inspired to immerse myself in Italian faith and tradition.

Sacred traditions permeate everyday living because Christianity landed in Roma as official and legal in 313 AD by Emperor Constantine. Apostles Peter and Paul brought their teachings of the New Testament after coming from Jerusalem and established the Roman Catholic Church. The Divine and sacred traditions founded in St. Peter's Catholic Church in Roma and the Pope's ever-presence in Vatican City reveal their supernatural faith in the Lord. A belief in power and will outside of themselves: God's will, God's higher law. I still hear my Nonna Antonia, "God-da knows!"

If one does not feel inspired by nearly 2000 years of Catholic spiritual practice within Roman *chiesa*, church walls and awaken to the presence and reverence for God, His Son, and the Holy Spirit in the Holy Trinity, then I weep in mercy for such a soul.

Italians are wholeheartedly devoted to their families fueled by customs and their Catholic faith. Even in recent times most Italians are baptized and wed in the Catholic Church. There is an integrated attitude in the important aspects of Christian values, living a Godly life.

Catholic rituals are still deeply rooted in the Italian psyche with as much as 90% considering themselves Roman Catholic even though not practicing the faith. Public schools, in previous years, offered religion as regular academic study. Now it is still an elective class once a week in public schools and is highly encouraged by parents and spiritual advisors. The fundamentals are God created our existence to preserve and be fruitful in the universe. We need to believe in God's law in order to realize we are free, by way of our free will to choose -- good or evil.

Many Catholics pray to the saints for special needs and talk of miracles--specialty saints. For example, pray to St. Francis of Assisi to watch over nature in your garden, pets, and wild animals. We still pray to the patron saint of travel, St. Christopher for safety on our journey or drive. If you've lost something a prayer to St. Anthony is often said, "Anthony, St. Anthony please come around: something is lost and cannot be found." Saints give their lives over to God fully and ask Him to lead them on a Godly path. Saints are surrounded in mystery by way of their experience with miracles, apparitions, humility, and graceful life. An investigation by the Vatican confirms their visions and miracles for canonization into sainthood.

Sunday is a day of rest as the Lord deemed -- a time for church and a time for family gathering. *Molto*, many families are immersed in their faith and religiously participate at the dinner table without television, pop music, phones, or media distraction. Families are united and surround themselves with the joys of nature at Sunday dinners spread outside on long tables and delectable meals. A long table seating up to twenty, covered by a white cotton tablecloth, and laden with fresh fruits and vegetables from the farm is where families lay to rest their digital devices and join in joyful, meaningful conversation. They are nurtured with Christian values as the groundwork for family and community stability and support.

The Sign of the Cross

Known as the Holy Trinity, in the Name of The Father, and of The Son, and of The Holy Spirit (Ghost) is my first lasting impression of Catholicism. The Holy Spirit is the love between Father and Son. This is the sign of the cross made symbolically across your chest as the beginning of a prayer. The fingers touch the forehead, pass to the middle of the sternum, cross over to the left shoulder, and back to the right shoulder (right-handed).

Principal Sister John Ann religiously ingrained this in my memory during the primary years at St. Pius X School, Denver, Colorado. I believe The Sisters of Charity changed it to Holy Spirit by the time I was ten or so. They realized it gave too many children a scary movie ghost connotation for reciting The Sign of the Cross.

Any reference to the Holy Ghost made these God-fearing Catholic children feel the fire and brimstone punishment was upon us. How did these simple, formative minds grasp the complexity of the spiritual love known as the Holy Spirit, between God in heaven and His Son Jesus Christ for man on earth, particularly in a Trinity of three united? Faith.

So petrified by the teachings of guilt and fear instilled by the Sisters of Charity, I already suffered from anxiety about it at age seven. I took it all in literally. When called upon to recite my Catechism Book answers, the teacher's favored method of testing, even after studying well, my brain would freeze and panic, without the ability to retrieve the answers. Consequently, my only D grade ever in school was second-grade religion. I pictured the Holy Ghost lurking round the next corner posed for confrontation, even for minor sins. From that point on, as a seven-year-old second grader, I already resigned myself from ever becoming a nun or saint.

Italians are comfortable in their identity with the greater purpose of God and eternity.

Find the courage and heart to research and relish your own national identity, gifts, and talents, born out of your ancestry. Resist those that discredit or homogenize your ethnicity. Stand fully proud of who you are, and the path of opportunity placed before you by your God-given talents. There is no greater individual worldly pursuit than blazing a trail for your future to instill character, moral identity, and prosperity of spirit and soul.

San Francisco Bay area has existed as a prime example of micro-cultures living respectfully in harmony under the umbrella of the city. While I lived there, many Italians resided in North Beach, Chinese and Asians in Chinatown, Hispanics in the Mission, LGBTQ in Castro, and African American in Oakland.

Italian faith fosters a sense of being, rather than having -- shining light on why those seeking material prosperity and pleasure for joy, eventually end in discontent and signifies how the Italian spirit is to be admired. How powerful simplicity and prayer can be. By placing God first in their lives, everything else falls into place. There is no situation that is helpless with Christ as their refuge.

The heart is at the core of your being and character. Italian's strong belief in forming Christian virtues from youth on is what helps build such magnificent character. They believe in heaven and hell, knowing there are eternal consequences. Such character in a country populated with over 60 million, supports over 60 million visitors as of 2018-2019. An astounding, almost overwhelming accomplishment, since they must accommodate more than their own population sometimes throughout the year and embrace these tourists are guests with all their character flaws.

Here are some astounding credits that I only recently discovered:

The first Catholic hospital was founded in Florence in the 1200s, Santa Maria Nuova. Catholic hospitals, clinics, and senior homes number approximately 15% of U.S. healthcare. Catholic hospitals are the largest non-government entity of healthcare.

Catholic charities provide the greatest relief for poverty and disaster next to government programs. Catholic schools account for 20% of U.S. schools. How this has been overlooked speaks volumes of those wishing for awards and humility, which is one of the most admired virtues in Catholicism.

There are more than 10,000 saints honored by the Roman Catholic Church, most designated by way of humility, prayerful life, and/or witnessing miracles throughout their life. Saints are elevated by their ability to recognize and summon Divine miracles, giving their lives over to the Lord and living a life of sacrifice and virtue. We honor them as we do our current heroes who dedicate their lives to a nobler, Godly cause. Many of the most popular saints celebrated today are Italian.

The glorious art, architecture, and religious symbols are visible on nearly every street throughout Italy, not simply in churches and museums by way of icons, relics, sculptures, and paintings. All this signifies adopting humility within their own lives knowing God has the ultimate control.

The more I study Italian tradition and heritage, the more I realize the significance of one's culture to feel a connection at home and at peace, knowing your place not only in the world but in eternity. Italians don't hesitate to make friends instantly through emotional and spiritual recognition.

Italians are preordained to believe without doubt and fear, their personal identity, within the family, community, and region that fills them with love. Such support systems based on traditions and values within the family create a long thriving life and content societies.

I remember the Italians spontaneously singing and playing instruments on their balconies, beating pots and pans for their neighbors to socialize during the start of COVID-19 seen on YouTube with such stage presence, you'd think they were on an opera stage as they communicate and entertain neighbors with such joy and spirit. If there's any good that came of COVID, one takeaway is that at home we all need to integrate our families at times, even at worktime--Like when the kids or dogs suddenly appear on your screen during a virtual meeting.

"I do it for the Lord," says the laborer who merrily sings across Piazza de la San Pietro of Vatican City when asked by a priest who greets him every day, how he stays so happy in his line of work. Their pride in service and manufacturing a product is not considered menial by any means in Italian society and flourishes amongst generations, whether crafting leather shoes, cobbling stones in the street, blowing glass, restoring art, or spinning silk. Italians often prefer labor in family artisan and service crafts because there is respect for these occupations with generations of expertise, versus an entry level white collar, college graduate office job as expected in the United States.

Perhaps our values will gravitate toward respect with this awareness and change from overconsumption and accumulation. The obvious cost of greed in our society and economic downfall brings us back to basics. The economic need can help restore harmony, productivity, and value in our everyday lives. Back to *il dolce far niente*, the sweetness of doing nothing, combined with a purpose in our American tradition. We may do well to emulate and build upon an Italian model of family.

Justice Antonin Scalia stated, "*...in America, to be Catholic sets you apart as being different.*"

We find spirit in our historical, ethnic, economic, and religious culture. You nurture your spirit by learning to further your aspirations to heaven by honoring moral values, traditions, Christian and religious landmarks. The barbaric elimination of tearing down statues and monuments or rewriting history because of those that foster power and corruption does not help others or history education.

Examine a painting by Raffaello who adores the Virgin Mary in many paintings surrounded by cherubs and angels winging. Blessed Mary with *bambini* Jesus brings out the Italian man's instilled adoration of women. Raffaello was born in Urbino, Le Marche where my paternal great-grandparents originated - helps explain my desire to be a Renaissance woman.

Amongst geniuses, Dante's "Divine Comedy" depicts the Christian Catholic levels of heaven, hell, and purgatory. The Italian language belongs to Dante. Machiavelli describes political issues of ethics. Famous Italian explorers include Cristoforo Columbo, Amerigo Vespucci, and Marco Polo amongst forty others navigating the world since the 13th Century. Astronomy discoveries reaching for the stars were born out of Galileo and the navigators. The stars highlight a perfect destiny in summing up Italian Divinity.

"Faith and reason are two wings on which the human spirit rises to the contemplation of truth." --Saint Pope John Paul

Faith and reason exist together intellectually. We use reason to discern truth.

Italian families surround themselves with icons, paintings, statues, and relics of a spiritual and God-given nature in nearly every avenue of living. Divine Destiny is the pulsebeat that breathes an energetic spirit in the faithful whose strong belief is that "Through God, all things are possible." The Roman Catholic Church honors eternity with an everlasting afterlife, where the motivation lies beyond our worldly life. The frequency of miracles over the centuries, experienced by both saints and sinners throughout Italy is plentiful, still unexplainable by science, and fully embraced by the faithful.

The Italian life foundation of faith, family and community can readily be observed:

Faith in God's laws, the soul, eternity

Family in unity, heart, and tradition

Friends in community, culture, and heritage

Look for the Italian spirit soaring on the wings of a dove. Now pause and listen…

hear a choir of Franciscan brothers chanting glorious prayers from their abbey, echoing about the stone walls. Hear the bells of numerous *campaniles,* towers tolling from hilltop towns in *armonia splendido,* harmony across the velvet green valleys. Happy melodic voices speak the Italian language in their favorite local *trattoria,* gathering at *passeggiate,* evening walks, and town piazzas.

You see in countless Renaissance paintings and sculptures, the grace of human anatomy, the period of humanism, formed from earth's raw materials that capture the Italian spirit in Divine art and architecture. Revere the portrayal of angels, saints, and the Lord in living miracles. Find the spirit in faith, family, community festivals, creative genius, and cultural identity.

Beauty and art can raise us up to a spiritual level, elevating the mind. Angels sing *Panis Angelicus,* bread of angels, as they harmonize an angelic aria. The Italian spirit rises with everlasting faith in truth and eternity. In Italy, you are surrounded in spirit –

The Italian Spirit.

A Portrait of Italy

A portrait of Italy whose chiseled features
Illuminate man's most magnificent creatures,
Donning a sturdy Neapolitan face,
Of olive complexion and eyes of grace
Eyes that tell of conquest, deep into the soul
Eyes for creation, set each artistic goal.

A Roman Profile with features for flair
Tumbling dark strands and wavy hair,
Fashion couture, with stunning and dare
Revealing layers of styles to wear

Lips pout and speak with smiles
Voices that carry for miles and miles
Voices that ring with drama and laughter
Voices that sing aria from here to thereafter
The genius for design, most succinct
The nose for opportunity most distinct
An ear for music most refined
A talent for creating most defined

Agreeable demeanor even out of text
Beaming promise one moment and heartbreak the next
Expressions extreme from terse to elated
Exhilarating happiness, community piazza congregated.

Oh, boot of Italy, so marched upon
Legs do carry this boot through dawn.
Worn these boots, worn on these feet
One wears a style of Italy, most complete.

Oh, heart of Italy my spirit, my soul, my home
Across your boot many regions I do roam
Families embrace me, welcome the saints
Italians' sacred spirit shines a golden dome.

Olive tree meander your branches of peace
Cypress-row soldiers stand and salute thee,
Descendants ever reaching in each branch,
Limbs extend through each piazza and village,
Italians, steeped in history, pageantry,
Roots through heritage of beauty and strength bred
Ancestry through ages where families have led.

A Portrait of Italy is Family, Faith, and Community

--*Nancy Mondi*

About Author

Since age 12, I was infatuated with Renaissance Art. After 23 years of admiring Italian art and culture, my passion for all things Italian was ignited watching *A Room with A View*, in 1988, consumed with an irresistible desire to get to Italy. Just eight months later, the adventure begins with a solo journey along the Mediterranean from Nice, France to Florence Italy, landing in my own room with a view not far from The Arno River. I was not a woman of independent means, just doggedly determined to reach my destination. There's no better feeling in the world than arriving at my room or a villa in Italy.

Years at 20th Century Fox Film helped develop my writing skills in creative advertising administration with copywriting in the 1980s. Forward 14 years, as I rush across the Golden Gate Bridge in 2003 headed to the San Francisco Ballet Academy in the heart of the city. I'm mentally dancing through my lesson plan with ballet steps in last-minute preparation with hands-on and off the steering wheel; jete', beat, beat, chasse' tour jete' run, run leap for the fourth and fifth-grade students at San Francisco Ballet Academy. It is in that inspired moment overlooking the grand city outline of San Francisco founded by Italian immigrants, that an Italian cultural connection is a story I must tell. I turn the rhythm of dance to the rhythm of writing.

A Bachelor of Arts Education at the University of Northern Colorado honed my teaching skills. A lifetime ballet background inspired me as a performer, instructor, and choreographer at Colorado Ballet Academy: in addition, to teaching for San Francisco Ballet Education and Bayer Ballet. Sixteen years were spent in San Francisco, Sausalito, and Sonoma until 2016. The vineyards reminded me of the Italian landscape, nurturing writing, and the influences of Italian descent.

My time in Palm Desert, 2005-2010, became dedicated to writing in the serenity of the California desert and became my retreat for 4 years, also serving as a Board Member of the Palm Springs Writers Guild.

I began writing this book fifteen years ago. A head injury in 2010 with PTSD caused an upheaval in my brain and thinking, so essentially, I had to reboot my brain and develop the finer cognitive skills again. Recovery required seven years with every breath of energy, learning to cope with daily routines, and feeling confident in writing again, and a few more years to recapture my sense of humor.

I now live north of Denver, my birthplace, in Loveland, Colorado near the foot of Rocky Mountain National Park since 2016, where the wildlife plays, enjoying outdoor activities and gardening with my husband Raymond and Westie dog, Madalena Serafina Valentina. Ray and I delight in beaches, baseball, and ballroom dance. We sing with joy in our church choir on Sundays, uplifted to The Divine.